The Horseman's Guide to Michigan Trails

HORSEMAN'S GUIDE TO MICHIGAN TRAILS

John Faitel

Horseman's Guide To Michigan Trails

Every effort has been made to supply complete and accurate information. However, JF Press assumes no responsibility for its use, nor for any infringement of the intellectual property rights of third parties which would result from such use. Neither the publisher, editor, compiler or contributors are responsible for errors or omissions in trail information; or for conditions and/or the sharing of trails; camping facilities or the lack thereof; bugs, flies, mosquitoes, or trail dust; overabundance or absence of wildlife; or any other conditions, situations or experiences of users of this guide. Maps are not to scale and should be used as a guide only.

Front cover photograph: Kate Coffey
Back cover photograph: Donald Hillman
Cover design: Diane Bareis

To Anna, who always loved horses.

ACKNOWLEDGEMENTS

Thanks are due to Beverly Grunheid for her suggestions, convictions and organizational information; to Pam Wingfield and Gail Firman for camping and trail information; to Cheryl Schram and John Snyder of *Equine Times* for trail information and locations; and to Marion Sinclair for her comments about trail descriptions.

Thanks also to Mark Mandenburg, Dean Sandell and Joseph Jarecki of the Michigan Department of Natural Resources for answering endless questions and giving quick responses.

And, last but not least, thanks also to Dolly Brock and Diane Bareis for all the finishing touches.

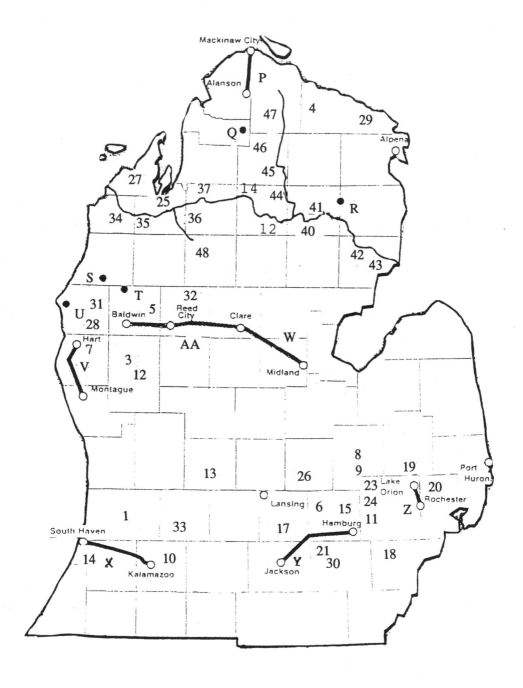

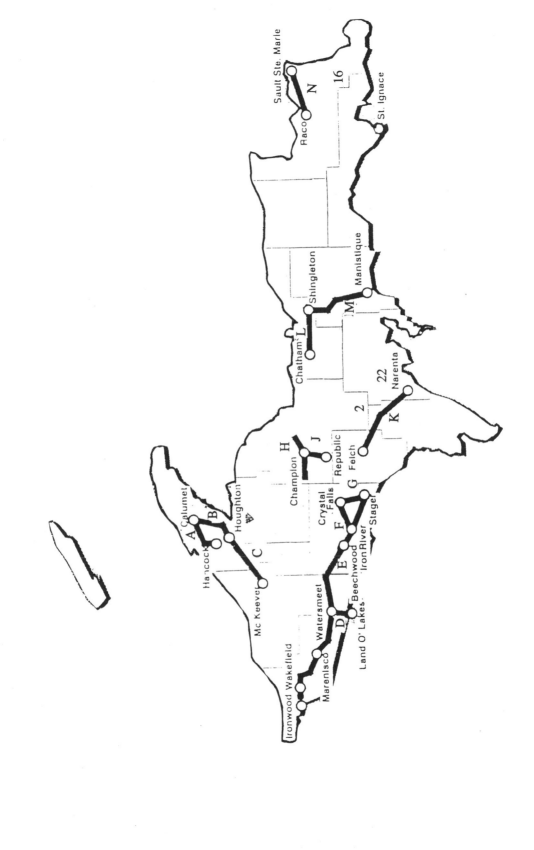

CONTENTS

SHORE-TO-SHORE TRAILS

RAILS TO TRAILS

A. HANCOCK/CALUMET TRAIL
    Hancock to Calumet
    Houghton County
    Original ballast; 12.5 miles

    Copper Country State Forest
    PO Box 440
    Baraga, MI 49908
    906-353-6651

B. KEWEENAW TRAIL
    Houghton to Calumet
    Houghton County
    Original ballast; 16 miles of 21 mile trail
    is abandoned ROW

    Copper Country State Forest
    PO Box 440
    Baraga, MI 49908
    906-353-6651

C. BILL NICHOLLS TRAIL
    McKeever to Houghton
    Ontonagan, Houghton Counties
    Original ballast; 40.6 miles of 55 mile
    trail is abandoned ROW

    Copper Country State Forest
    PO Box 440
    Baraga, MI 49908
    906-353-6651

D. WATERSMEET/LAND O'LAKES
    TRAIL
    Watersmeet to Land O'Lakes (WI)
    Gogebic County
    Original ballast; 8 miles

    US Forest Service
    PO Box 276
    Watersmeet, MI 49969
    906-358-4551

E. STATE LINE TRAIL
    Marenisco east to Stager
    Iron, Gogebic Counties
    Original ballast, 87.1 miles

    Marenisco west to Wakefield
    Gogebic County
    Original ballast; 15 miles of 20 mile trail
    is abandoned ROW

    Copper Country State Forest
    PO Box 440
    Baraga, MI 49908
    906-353-6651

F. CRYSTAL FALLS TO IRON RIVER
    TRAIL
    Iron County
    Original ballast, 25 miles

    Copper Country State Forest
    PO Box 440
    Baraga, MI 49908
    906-353-6651

G. CRYSTAL FALLS TO STAGER TRAIL
    Iron County
    Original ballast, 11 miles

    Copper Country State Forest
    PO Box 440
    Baraga, MI 49908
    906-353-6651

H. PESHEKEE TO CLOWRY ORV TRAIL
    Near Champion
    Marquette County
    Original ballast; 6.1 miles

    Ishpeming Forest Area
    Escanaba River State Forest
    1985 US 41
    Ishpeming, MI 49849
    906-485-1031

J. REPUBLIC/CHAMPION GRADE
    TRAIL
    Champion to Republic
    Marquette County
    Original ballast; 8 miles

    Ishpeming Forest Area
    Escanaba River State Forest
    1985 US 41
    Ishpeming, MI 49849
    906-485-1031

K. FELCH GRADE TRAIL
    Narenta to Felch
    Menominee, Delta, Dickinson Counties
    Original ballast, 27.5 miles of 45 miles
    trail is on abandoned ROW

    Norway Forest Area
    Copper Country State Forest
    US 2
    Norway, MI 49870
    906-563-9247

L. COALWOOD TRAIL
    Haywire Trail at Shingleton to Chatham
    Alger County
    Original ballast; 24 miles

    Shingleton Forest Area
    Lake Superior State Forest
    M-28
    Shingleton, MI 49884
    906-452-6227

M. HAYWIRE TRAIL
    Manistique to Shingleton
    Schoolcraft, Alger Counties
    Original ballast, 36 miles

    Hiawatha National Forest
    400 E. Munising
    Munising, MI 49862
    906-387-2512

N. SOO/STRONGS TRAIL
    Sault Ste. Marie west to Raco
    Chippewa County
    Original ballast; 16.7 miles of 20 miles
    trail is abandoned ROW

    Lake Superior State Forest
    PO Box 798
    Sault Ste. Marie, MI 49783
    906-293-5131

Raco west to Strongs
Chippewa County
Original ballast, 12.3 miles

Hiawatha National Forest
4000 I-75 Business Loop
Sault Ste. Marie, MI 49783
906-635-5311

P. MACKINAW/ALANSON TRAIL
    Mackinaw to Alanson
    Emmet, Cheboygan County
    Original ballast; 24 miles

    Mackinaw State Forest
    PO Box 660
    Gaylord, MI 49735
    517-732-3541

Q. SPRING BROOK PATHWAY
    Jordan River State Forest &
    Mackinaw State Forest
    Charlevoix County
    Original ballast; .75 miles of 6.25 miles
    trail is abandoned ROW

    Gaylord Field Office
    PO Box 667
    Gaylord, MI 49735
    517-732-3571

R. HURON FOREST
    SNOWMOBILE TRAILS
    Huron National Forest
    Alcona, Oscoda Counties
    Natural materials; 11 miles of 95 mile
    trail is abandoned ROW

    Harrisville Ranger District
    Huron National Forest
    PO Box 286
    Harrisville, MI 48740
    517-724-6471

S. BIG "M" CROSS
    COUNTRY SKI TRAIL
    Manistee National Forest
    Manistee County
    Native materials, .75 miles of 18.6 mile
    trail is abandoned ROW

    US Forest Service
    1658 Manistee Highway
    Manistee, MI 59440
    616-723-2211

T. IRON'S AREA TOURIST
ASSOCIATION SNOWMOBILE TRAIL
Manistee National Forest
Lake, Manistee Counties
Original ballast; 22 miles

US Forest Service
1658 Manistee Highway
Manistee, MI 59440
616-723-2211

U. NORDHOUSE DUNES
TRAIL SYSTEM
Manistee National Forest
Nordhouse Dunes Wilderness
Mason County
Sand; 4 miles of 15 mile trail is
abandoned ROW

US Forest Service
1658 Manistee Highway
Manistee, MI 59440
616-723-2211

V. HART-MONTAGUE BICYCLE TRAIL
STATE PARK
Hart to Montague
Oceana, Muskegon Counties
Asphalt; 22.5 miles

Silver Lake State Park
Route 1, Box 254
Mears, MI 49436
616-873-3083

W. PERE MARQUETTE RAIL-TRAIL OF
MID-MICHIGAN
Midland to Clare
Midland, Isabella Counties
Crushed stone; 26.5 miles when
completed; total trail 30 miles

Midland County Parks Recreation Dept.
220 W. Ellsworth St.
Midland, MI 48640-5194
517-832-6870

X. KAL-HAVEN TRAIL
SESQUICENTENNIAL STATE PARK
Kalamazoo to South Haven
Kalamazoo, VanBuren Counties
Crushed stone; 34.1 miles

Van Buren State Park
23960 Ruggles Rd..
South Haven, MI 49090
616-637-4984

Y. LAKELANDS TRAIL STATE PARK
Jackson to Hamburg (West Unit)
South Lyon to Wixom (East Unit)
Jackson, Ingham, Livingston, Oakland
counties
Original ballast; 29 miles west unit; 7
miles east unit; 36 miles total

Pinckney Recreational Area
8555 Silver Hill, Route 1
Pinckney, MI 48169
313-426-4913

Z. PAINT CREEK TRAIL
Lake Orion to Rochester
Oakland County
Crushed limestone; 10.5 miles

Paint Creek Trailways Commission
4393 Collins Rd..
Rochester, MI 49064
313-651-9260

AA. PERE MARQUETTE (EXTENSION)
Clare, Osceola, Lake Counties
54 miles
Scheduled to open by 1996

MICHIGAN'S SHORE-TO-SHORE
RIDING-HIKING TRAIL

Michigan's Shore-To-Shore Trail stretches some 220 miles from the Lake Michigan shore on the west to the shore of Lake Huron on the east. Its route across the northern Lower Peninsula traverses some of the most scenic country in the state. Part of the trail parallels beautiful rivers. Its path lies through stately pines and hardwoods, along forest trails and scenic highways. Public trail camps, as well as private facilities and services, are available for trail users.

The Michigan Trail Riders Association was organized with the primary purpose of establishing and maintaining the Shore-To-Shore Riding-Hiking Trail and its camps. For more information on goals, trail rides and membership in MTRA, send a self-addressed, stamped envelope to:

Michigan Trail Riders Association, Inc.
1650 Ormond Rd..
White Lake, MI 48383

You must be a member 30 days prior to any scheduled ride to participate with the MTRA. The tentative ride schedule for 1996 includes:

May 11-19	Blossom Ride
June 1-9	Shore-To-Shore
June 15-30	Shore to Shore
August 5-24	Double Cross
August 10-18	Summer Ride
September 5-15	Shore To Shore
September 15-24	Shore-To-Shore
October 5-13	Color Ride

Shore-To-Shore Trails are listed in the Table of Contents.

FOREWORD

This book evolved from a need for a horseman's guide to the horse trails in Michigan. The information herein was compiled from resources including the Michigan Department of Natural Resources, the United States Forest Service, county governments, Michigan Trail Riders Association, The Rails To Trails Conservancy, private business and individuals with a love of horses and trail riding.

We have tried to include all of the "open to the public" riding areas in Michigan. If we have missed one of your riding areas, please drop us a note and it will be included in the next edition.

As horsepeople, we should remember those who work on our behalf to keep trails open. We should support their labors with our time and effort, our money and our votes.

This guide lists 15 trail camps developed since the early 1960s by the Michigan Trail Riders Association (MTRA), a non-profit organization whose prime purpose is to establish and maintain the Shore-To-Shore Horse Trail and Camps. As trail riders, we owe a heartfelt thanks to those members, past and present, who have worked for the benefit of all trail users.

TRAIL RIDING
by C. Melvin Bradley

More and more families are having fun trail riding. This activity is reasonably inexpensive, is non-competitive, and affords relaxation on nature's scenic trails. Many individuals seek trail riding as a hobby in their retirement. They enjoy many acquaintances from past years and look forward to making new ones on each day's ride. Many youngsters also enjoy the responsibility of a horse or pony as they ride with their families. This helps them grow up to appreciate the contribution a horse can make to their development. And the natural surroundings of scenic trails provide a most enjoyable setting.

INTERMEDIATE TRAIL RIDING

Intermediate trail riding is considered to be of more than one day's duration. The ride may be arranged for and sponsored by a local group or it may be a commercial trail ride. Each year more commercial rides are available to our nation's riders.

A ride may range up to a week or more in length and cover 15 to 40 miles a day in a continuous direction. In this case, some provision is made to bring the riders' equipment forward each day from the previous night's camp to the new location.

The ride may start from and return to a central camp site each day. For this ride, the camping equipment remains at a central location. Large groups may have an all-day "fast" ride and an all-day "slow" ride, along with a half-day "fast" ride and a half-day "slow" ride.

SELECTING THE RIDE

A ride should be judged on scenic beauty, accommodations, and cost. Before committing for a week's ride, ask questions of someone who has been on the ride. Ask about the terrain, how far they ride each day, how many hours are ridden daily and what kind of housing you need.

Clear, cold water running through meadows with tree-fringed banks nearly always appeals to trail riders. If the terrain allows, a stream may be crossed many times in a day's ride. A ride may go upstream the opposite side in the afternoon. During the process, they may cross the stream some ten or twelve times. Streams can be combined with rough country to give scenic beauty and add interest to the ride. The most interesting scenes should be used as lunch sites or rest stops.

Hill and mountain riding can be popular when carefully selected. They can be challenging to horse and rider. Hill riding in heavy timber may not be fun because of little air circulation in warm climates. For this reason you may wish to ride in the hills during the cool, color season of autumn or in the spring.

It is important when riding in the fall to take rain clothes along, because if you get wet it can be very chilling before the end of the day.

Some rides can be arranged through areas of wildlife preserves and areas where game can be seen. A ride where wild turkey or deer can be seen adds interest and some thrills.

Fragrance of pine trees following a shower is always enjoyed by trail riders. The remoteness and quietness of riding through pine forests meets with great favor.

CONSIDER CAMP ACCOMMODATIONS

Consider facilities of the camp from which you are going to make the ride. Most commercial camp sites have electrical service in areas offering shade. Pickup campers, travel trailers, and tents are the living units of most trail riders. A large camp may accommodate 1,500 riders, have miles of electrical wiring, a large cooking and dining tent, and a horse show arena.

Most riders appreciate a hot meal delivered to them at a designated spot for the noon lunch. The fare should be adequate, with two or three kinds of drinks available. It should also be scenically located.

Consider other accommodations for the ride. Check for bath or shower accommodations.

Additional recreational opportunities may accompany some rides. Some people enjoy swimming their horses at the end of a long ride after they have cooled them out. This is a good sport, but it can be dangerous if not handled properly. If your horse is not an experienced swimmer, use a neck rope. Some horses will rear when they get in deep water before they begin swimming. A rope gives the rider protection. If dislodged and hit on the head by the horse's knee or foot, the temporary incapacitation may result in drowning. Always have someone with you when swimming a horse.

A good change of pace for riders is to come in early and take a canoe trip. Where streams have a reasonable amount of current, a trip of several miles can be taken in a few hours. There may be operators who will rent canoes and pick up canoers downstream at predesignated locations.

Most youngsters and many adults enjoy a dance at night after trail riding. Some rides furnish bands and a dance floor for entertainment. However, riders who like to sleep early may not enjoy "pop bands" and dance floors near where they camp.

Many trail rides have organized horse shows with a variety of classes, including a number of fun classes. Remember, the main purpose of the trail ride is to have fun. People who get "uptight" about winning a horse show should leave showing for another occasion.

Most rides offer church services on Sunday. Some people even go so far as getting married on their horses on trail rides.

TYPE OF HORSE FOR TRAIL RIDING

Most any type, size, age, and quality of horse can be seen on large trail rides. This is one reason trail riding is popular, there is no competition and no rivalry between riders as they follow the trail over scenic trails. Serious trail riders, however, usually agree on broad generalities to describe a good trail horse.

Generally speaking, a good trail horse is large enough to carry the rider well. He is soft in his gaits for his breed, with more than average speed at the walk. He should travel with a purpose. He should be willing to keep up with the other horses without charging upon their heels. He should be safe to ride, willing to cross all of the obstacles, be surefooted, and require a minimum of guidance from the rider. Further, he should be disease-resistant and should not be accident-prone. On large trail rides perhaps there are fewer than 10 percent of the horses of this description.

Avoid dangerous horses that may buck or run away, or those that intentionally kick other horses and people. Since much of the riding is done at a walk, a horse should be able and willing to stride along and travel at a rate of about four miles an hour. When most of the horses in a line are walking and your horse has to jog or trot most of the time to keep up, you may be in need of a different horse. On the other hand, you don't want a "prancy," "chargey" horse that will not settle down and walk.

There is a lot of difference in the weight-carrying ability of horses. Some horses should be rested every other day. Others can carry a rider every day. Generally speaking, horses should not asked to carry much more than 20 or 25 percent of their body weight. Weights above this amount are tiresome to most horses.

CONDITIONING YOURSELF AND YOUR HORSE

Conditioning yourself and your horse is important before serious trail riding. Although some riders condition their horses at slow speeds on trail rides, generally speaking horses need forced exercise. It may take a minimum of three weeks to get a horse ready for a trail ride. A fat horse may need about four or five weeks of reduced feed and increased riding to get in condition. Young horses require more time.

Proper conditioning may include a half hour's ride a day the first few days, increased to an hour or more daily one week later, finally increased to two hours. By the end of the conditioning period, a daily ride of about half the distance of an average day on the trail is sufficient. Two horses can be conditioned at the same time by riding one and leading the other.

For a horse that is too thin for serious trail riding, increase the feed and exercise to gain more conditioning before the ride. A horse will likely lose weight while on a ride.

Don't allow your horse's feet to get in poor condition. If the shoe is left on too long, the heels overgrow it and extend down over the branches to the shoe. This can cause germs and other serious foot problems. Remove shoes before they reach this point and either reshoe or trim the feet for going barefoot.

Have your horse shod ten days to three weeks ahead of the ride. This allows the sole time to thicken and the wall time to grow down enough to get the horse's feet up off the rocks. If correction is needed, it gives the owner time to do so before leaving home. Such correction might be recovery from a nail prick, interfering, or discovery that the horse needs pads.

EQUIPMENT FOR TRAIL RIDING

The type of equipment for trail rides depends on the type of ride, weather conditions, and accessibility of the trail. It is usually best to take along your own grain rather than buy it on the ride because the horse is used to eating it. He may go off his feed or get colic if feed is changed. Because of inconvenience of hauling hay, it is usually best to buy it on the ride. A box or pan is needed for feeding grain. Pans that stack together require much less space in transportation. To feed the appropriate amount, take along the measure used at home.

Hay feeders are convenient for trail riding. The sash cord type tends to twist and makes filling difficult. Those with rings at the top do not twist and are easier to open and close for convenience in filling.

Take along neck ropes. These should be strong, longer than usual and soft enough to stay tied easily. A neck rope 12 feet long allows tying around a rather large tree. Use a halter with a neck rope to keep the horse from being choked if he pulls back hard.

Take adequate saddle blankets on a trail ride. Horses ridden hard should have 1½ inches of padding under their saddles. This requires a saddle with a wide enough gullet to accommodate thick padding. Some pad materials pick up many weed seeds. Padding can be alternated daily to provide dryness and protection for a hard-working horse.

Many large trail rides have horseshoers available. If your horse requires corrective shoeing, take along an extra set of shoes. Some horses need trailers behind and pads in front.

Carry water on rides in hot weather. A quart canteen is preferred if it will supply enough water, because it will bounce less in saddlebags if you are traveling with much speed. A half-gallon container has sufficient weight to pull saddlebags sideways and bounce but is not necessary for long, dry rides.

Not every rider in a party needs this much equipment. But one in almost all parties does. Saddlebags are convenient to carry the canteen, neck rope, slicker, hoof pick, camera or other items. Some riders have wire cutters, which are most convenient if a horse gets tangled in loose wire. On the other hand, park managers and landowners are skeptical of riders who indiscriminately use wire cutters.

Consider these additional items for your trail ride: an extra cinch, breast collar, cinch strap, curb strap, picket line and rake. The picket line can also be used to load reluctant horses, and a rake is convenient to rake droppings away from the horse's bedding area.

If you have a handyman in the crowd, he may wish to bring a few other items. Saddle soap and a sponge should be available, because you are likely to get your saddle wet crossing streams or riding in the rain. Application of saddle soap will restore items and prevent them from drying out.

Consider some items of medication for your horse. He may need something for abrasions or open wounds. Fly repellent and a thermometer are also recommended items. Many times, especially during early spring, viruses or bacterial outbreaks will go through horses that are bunched together. If your horse's temperature at rest is much over 102 degrees, he should be rested that day.

If you are susceptible to poison ivy, chiggers or other vectors, you may wish to take along some first aid medication.

HAULING TO THE RIDE

Have solid footing in the bottom of your trailer, such as a mat. If you have a horse that pulls back and tends to have his back feet slip forward, put a one-inch oak cleat across the mat. This will help him keep from getting down and will aid him in getting up should he lose his footing.

Feed your horses loose in the trailer while you are training them to become familiar with it. Older horses should be fed in a trailer once in awhile.

Check your hitch. A high percentage of trailer accidents result from the trailer coming loose from the automobile. Be sure your hitch is tight and strong. If the ball is not welded, double-nut and use a heavy chain secured around the frame. If the hitch should fall, the chain should maintain control of the trailer until you could get stopped. All two-horse trailers should have brakes, and in most states they are required by law.

Load the heavy horse on the left in a trailer. This is because roads are higher in the center than on the outside, and you have more control of a load with the weight on the upper side. Give your horse head room. Sixteen hand horses need seven-foot tall trailers.

If the weather is cold, blanket your horse. It may even be necessary to close in most of the trailer in winter. On the other hand, if you unload and find the horses wet from perspiration under the blanket, don't use it under similar conditions next time.

Consider tying the horse securely with a slip-knot in the hope that it could be easily released. It might be all right to haul old, experienced horses in trailers without tying their heads, but in case they get down they can right themselves much easier if their heads are securely tied.

Be sure your direction lights are working. Check them along with brake lights and tail lights for night driving. Drive slowly the first few miles until you get a feel for the rig you are driving.

LOCATING YOUR SITE IN CAMP

When you arrive in camp, pick your camp site carefully. Most campers like to camp near a river for its scenic beauty and convenience of watering horses. Horseflies are worse along a stream than a quarter of a mile away from it.

Consider the tying opportunities for your horses and the quietness of your location. The quietest spot may be on the edge of the camp, and the noisiest near the center of activities such as a horse show arena or dance floor. Avoid camping near road junctions where there will be more traffic, both mounted and vehicles. Last but not least, consider convenience to facilities.

Remember the reason for trail riding is to have fun, so try to avoid inconveniences and accidents. Tie your horses securely. A good idea is using a neck rope with the shank run through the ring in the halter. When tied securely to a picket line this method is about as secure as any. While older, experienced trail horses will seldom leave camp, young horses on their first ride may be hopelessly lost if they get loose and try to go home.

ON THE TRAIL

Get up early enough in the morning to get your horse cleaned up, watered and fed grain at least an hour and a half before time to ride. Let him stand and eat hay as he wishes. Be sure your neck rope, hoof pick and water container are in the saddlebags.

Listen carefully to directions before making the day's ride. Dismount at refreshment stops. This allows your horse time to relax a bit and relieve his back from your weight and reduce the chance of a sore back.

A lunch stop affords an opportunity to rest your horse approximately one hour. Find a cool, shady spot if you can. Loosen the saddle cinch and tie him with the neck rope where he can't twist himself into tree branches. Most horses are not fed at the lunch hour.

Tie your horse on a short rein. Horses tied with long reins may be tangled in their reins, possibly leading to severe injury in the struggle. Also, this invites the horse to pull back.. Such tying is an invitation to trouble.

A thirsty horse will want to drink at first chance. It is usually considered safe to let a horse drink a substantial amount if he is going to continue to be ridden. However, gorging from cold mountain streams can cause convulsions and can actually cause death. For this reason it is better to allow a horse under these conditions to drink only five or six swallows of water. Let him drink more when he has had time to cool.

SAFETY PRECAUTIONS

A red ribbon tied to the tail of the horse indicates he is a kicker. Ride back away from these horses. If crowded they can severely injure you or your horse. Be sure to lead your horse sufficient distance away from tied horses that are prone to kick so you can't be reached by their heels. Sometimes they will charge and kick, especially if in camp where they are used to eating.

24

Saddles have a way of turning in the most inconvenient places. Sometimes saddles will turn because they are not cinched tightly enough. More than likely they will turn because the horse is fat and thick at the withers or the saddle is too narrow in the gullet, or for both reasons.

A horse with extreme thickness in the withers needs a saddle with a wide gullet and should always be ridden with a breast collar.

The temptation to ride sideways is great at the end of a hard day's ride. It may be restful to the rider, but it causes uneven pressure on the bars of the saddle that may give the horse a sore back.

FEEDING YOUR HORSE

When you return to camp, tie your horse on a picket line and give him a full feed of hay. It may be well to leave saddles on for half an hour to an hour. If a hot horse is uncinched and unsaddled immediately, blood may rush into the veins under the saddle and cause puffs and knots. Offer a feed of grain 1½ hours after cooling, watering and eating hay on the picket line. Feed grain again before going to bed, then in the morning 1½ hours before the ride starts. Feed hay free choice while the horse is in camp.

PRACTICE COURTESY

All riders should practice trail courtesy. While it may be fun to race through streams and splash water all over your friends, this could result in grim consequences if a young horse should run away or throw its rider.

Don't litter the scenic trails. If you are conducting a ride, always bring trash containers to collect empty bottles, cans and litter. Carry trash with you until you get to a stop, either in a saddlebag or in your pocket. Do not throw cigarettes aside. Remember most trail riders are guests, either of private landowners or on public property. It is to the benefit of everyone to be considerate and to keep trails clean.

1 ALLEGAN STATE GAME AREA
Allegan County

The Allegan County State Game Area of 45,000 acres was created in 1964 by the Michigan Department of Natural Resources to provide recreation for everyone with an outdoor interest. Special use areas for dog sleds and horseback riding have been designated on four distinct locations. Parking is along the side of the road in the riding areas. There are no designated horseback trails.

For information:
Game Area Headquarters
4590 118th Ave.
Allegan, MI 49010
(Mail inquiries should include a self-addressed, stamped envelope)

No fee

Directions: 120th Ave. and 51st St., Allegan County.

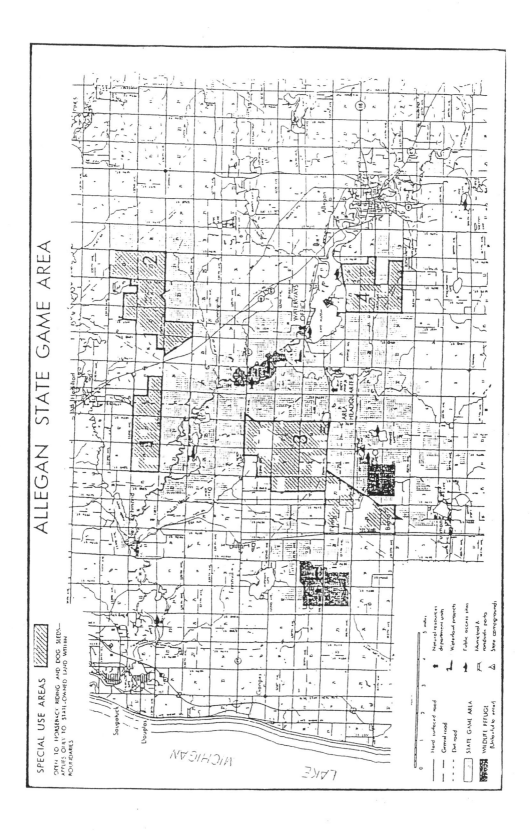

ALLEGAN STATE GAME AREA

27

	BAY DE NOC	
2	**GRAND ISLAND TRAIL** Genesse & Lapeer Counties - near Flint	

The Bay de Noc - Grand Island Trail parallels the Whitefish River, staying from .5 to 2 miles east of the river. The trail follows the approximate location of an ancient Chippewa Indian portage route used to carry canoes and supplies between Lake Superior and Lake Michigan. Following the river bluff for a considerable distance, it offers the rider many extended views to the west across the Whitefish River Valley. The southern quarter of the trail winds through pine, aspen, maple, birch and beech forests with short rounded hills and flat stretches.

Note: It is requested you protect the lakes and streams by 1) picketing horses at least 100 feet from the waters edge; 2) dismantle temporary hitch rails; 3) scatter the horse manure to discourage flies; and as camping courtesy to others, 4) pack-in, pack-out, as always.

Horsemen's facilities:
>   Large assembly area (three)
>   Picket areas
>   Water
>   Toilets
>   Rustic camping in the assembly areas
>   Approximately 40 miles of trail

For information:
>   Hiawatha National Forest
>   Rapid River Ranger District
>   Rapid River, MI 49878
>   906-474-6442

No fee

Directions: The Bay de Noc - Grand Island Trail begins from a point 2.25 miles east of the town of Rapid River and 1.0 miles north of US 2 and extends northward for about 40 miles, terminating at its intersection with State Road 94 at Ackerman Lake. The three mail trailheads are: Access A: 2.0 miles east of Rapid River on US 2 turn left on County Road 509 and travel 1.5 miles north. Parking lot is on west side of road. Trail goes north 22 miles to Access B. Access B: 2.0 miles east of Rapid River on US 2 turn left on County Road 509 and travel 16.0 miles north. Parking lot is on east side of road. Trail goes north 18 miles to Access C. Access B is best suited for camping because of its large space and quiet location off of County Road 509. Access C: Ten miles southwest of Munising on M-94. Parking lot is on north side of road opposite Ackerman Lake.

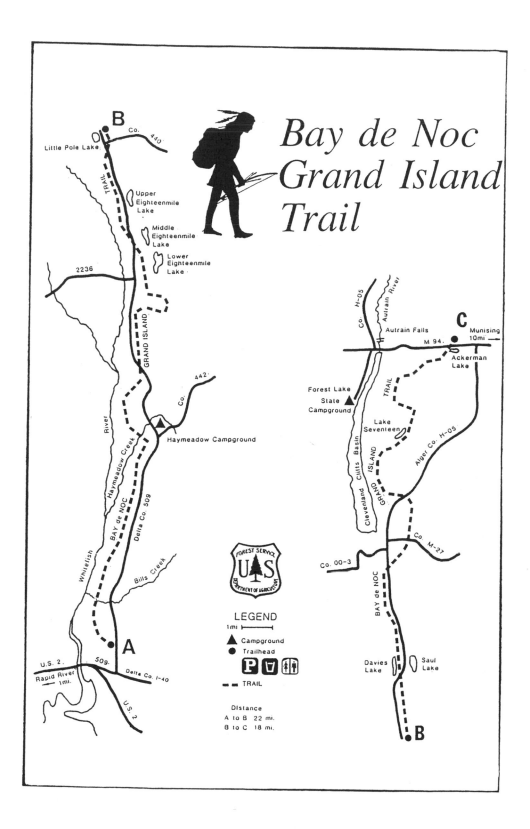

Bay de Noc Grand Island Trail

B

Little Pole Lake

Co. 440

Upper Eighteenmile Lake

Middle Eighteenmile Lake

Lower Eighteenmile Lake

2236

TRAIL

GRAND ISLAND

Co. 442

River

Haymeadow Creek

Haymeadow Campground

BAY de NOC

Delta Co. 509

Whitefish

Bills Creek

U.S. 2

Rapid River 1 mi.

509

Delta Co. I-40

A

U.S. 2

Co. H-05

Autrain River

Autrain Falls

M 94

Munising 10 mi

C

Ackerman Lake

Forest Lake State Campground

TRAIL

Lake Seventeen

Alger Co. H-05

Cleveland Cliffs Basin

GRAND ISLAND

Co. M-27

Co. 00-3

BAY de NOC

Davies Lake

Saul Lake

B

FOREST SERVICE
U S
DEPARTMENT OF AGRICULTURE

LEGEND

1 mi ├────┤

▲ Campground

● Trailhead

🅿 ⛺ 🚻

- - - TRAIL

Distance
A to B 22 mi.
B to C 18 mi.

BIGELOW CREEK
MANISTEE NATIONAL FOREST
Newaygo County - northeast of Newaygo

3

This is an 80-acre parcel on both sides of Bigelow Creek. Horsemen enjoy camping and riding here because of the natural beauty of the area.

Considerations:
1) No-trace camping; 2) Human waste must be buried 8 inches deep and away from camp, trails or water; 3) Use biodegradable soap and dispose of waste water at least 200 feet from any water source; 4) Keep fires safe and small; 5) Use only dead or fallen wood; 6) Remain on trail.

Horsemen's facilities:
Rustic camping
Horsemen may ride on any public roads and two-tracks

For information:
District Ranger
White Cloud Ranger District
PO Box 127
White Cloud, MI 49349
616-689-6696
800-821-6263

No fee

Directions: From M-37 in Newaygo, go east on Croton-Hardy Drive about 3.5 miles to Barberry Rd. Go left (north) about 1 mile to 58th St. Turn left (west) and go .75 to 1 mile to a two-track on the right (south) and turn into the camping area.

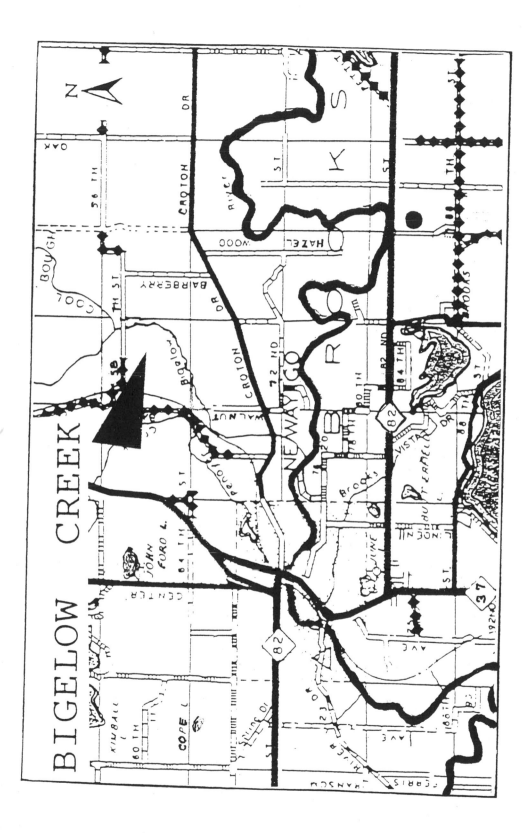

31

4 BLACK MOUNTAIN FOREST RECREATION AREA
Cheboygan and Presque Isle - north of Onaway

Horseback riding the two-track roads through the flats and over the hills of the Black Mountain Area has been popular for a long time. An abundance of oak trees are an element to the rich habitat for deer, squirrels, bear and turkeys which may be seen in the area. Trail riders will travel through a number of forest types and will see a managed forest in its various stages of regrowth and maturity.

Horsemen's facilities:
  5 rustic campsites
  Water
  Toilets
  Marked ORV routes or trails
  Miles of unmarked two-track roads and fire lanes
  Group camping by reservation

For information:
  Mackinaw State Forest
  PO Box 667
  Gaylord, MI 49735
  517-732-3541

Directions: From I-75 Exit 310 go east on M-68 about 8.25 miles to M-33. Turn left (north) about 9.2 miles to Mann Rd. Go right (east) about 5 miles to F05 (Gaynor Rd.), then left (north) about 2 miles to Twin Lakes Rd. Then right about 3 miles to Doriva Beech Rd. and turn left (north) about .4 miles to the horse camp on the right.

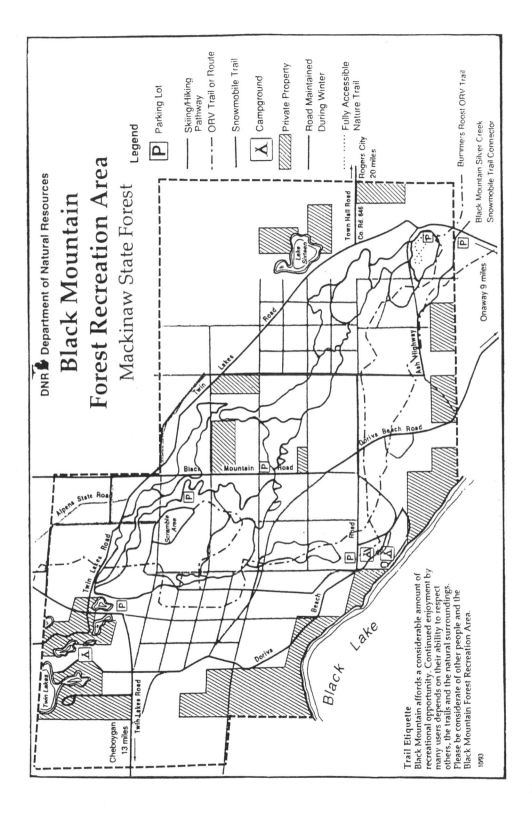

DNR ♣ Department of Natural Resources

Black Mountain
Forest Recreation Area
Mackinaw State Forest

Legend

P	Parking Lot
——	Skiing/Hiking Pathway
—·—·	ORV Trail or Route
——	Snowmobile Trail
🏕	Campground
▨	Private Property
——	Road Maintained During Winter
······	Fully Accessible Nature Trail

Rogers City 20 miles

Burnmer's Roost ORV Trail

Black Mountain Silver Creek Snowmobile Trail Connector

Onaway 9 miles

Town Hall Road

Co. Rd. 646

Ash Highway

Doriva Beach Road

Lake Sixteen

Lakes Road

Twin Lakes Road

Alpena State Road

Black Mountain Road

Scramble Area

Road

Beach

Doriva

Black Lake

Twin Lakes

Cheboygan 13 miles

Twin Lakes Road

Trail Etiquette

Black Mountain affords a considerable amount of recreational opportunity. Continued enjoyment by many users depends on their ability to respect others, the trails and the natural surroundings. Please be considerate of other people and the Black Mountain Forest Recreation Area.

1093

5	**BOWMAN LAKE AREA** **MANISTEE NATIONAL FOREST** Lake County - West of Baldwin	

Bowman Lake Area is a moderate-sized recreational area where you may experience solitude and closeness to nature. Interaction with other forest users in this area is generally infrequent. Glacial depressions and unique vegetation are found in this area and provide homes for many species of wildlife.

Considerations: 1) No-trace camping; 2) Human waste must be buried 8 inches deep and away from camp, trails or water; 3) Use biodegradable soap and dispose of waste water at least 200 feet from any water source; 4) Keep fires safe and small; 5) Use only dead or fallen wood; 6) Remain on trail.

Horseman's facilities:
Rustic camping area
Marked trail
Maps available

For information:
Forest Ranger
Baldwin Ranger District
Baldwin, MI 49304
616-745-3100
800-821-6263

No fee

Directions: From Baldwin, take 7th St. (52nd St.) west about 7 miles to the trailhead.

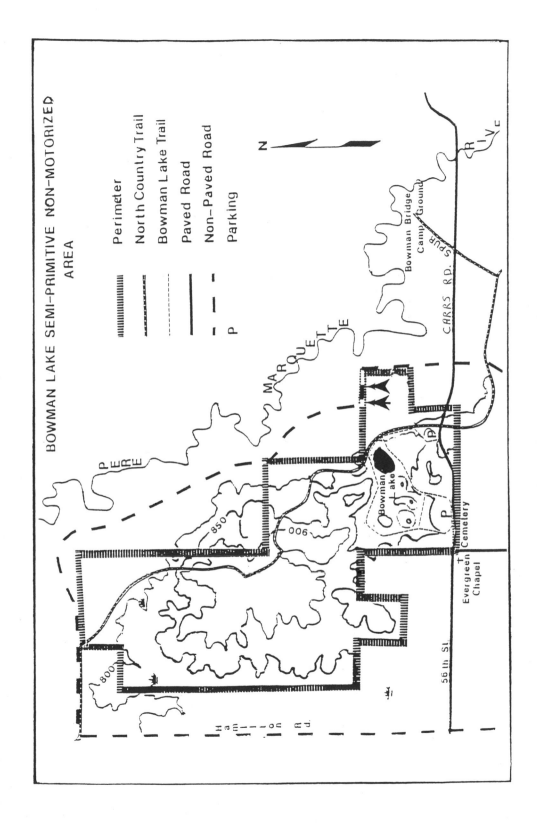

BOWMAN LAKE SEMI-PRIMITIVE NON-MOTORIZED AREA

Perimeter
North Country Trail
Bowman Lake Trail
Paved Road
Non-Paved Road
P   Parking

N

MARQUETTE

PERE

Bowman Lake

Bowman Bridge Camp Ground

CARRS RD.

SPUR

Evergreen Cemetery

Chapel

56th St.

Hamilton Rd.

850

900

800

35

This 4,940 acre State Recreation Area has a combination of high, irregular ranges of hills interspersed with a number of attractive lakes. Oak forest, thick hedge rows and open space blend on the uplands while grassy marshes, shrub masses and dense swamp are in are the lowlands. The horse trails skirt Shanango Lake and offer steep ridges and scenic views.

Horsemen's facilities:
Day use staging area
25 rustic campsites
Water
Toilets
18 miles of unmarked trails
Public riding stables 810-227-4622

For information:
Park Manager
Brighton Recreation Area
6360 Chilson Road
Howell, MI 48843
Tel: 810-229-6566
Fax: 810-229-2651

Fee

Directions: From I-96 just west of US 23, take Exit 147 (Spencer Road) and go west through Brighton on Brighton Road about 4 miles to Chilson Road. Turn left (south) to Bishop Lake Road. Turn right (west) to staging area or horse camp. The riding stables are further south on Chilson Road, about .25 miles on the right.

BRIGHTON STATE RECREATION AREA

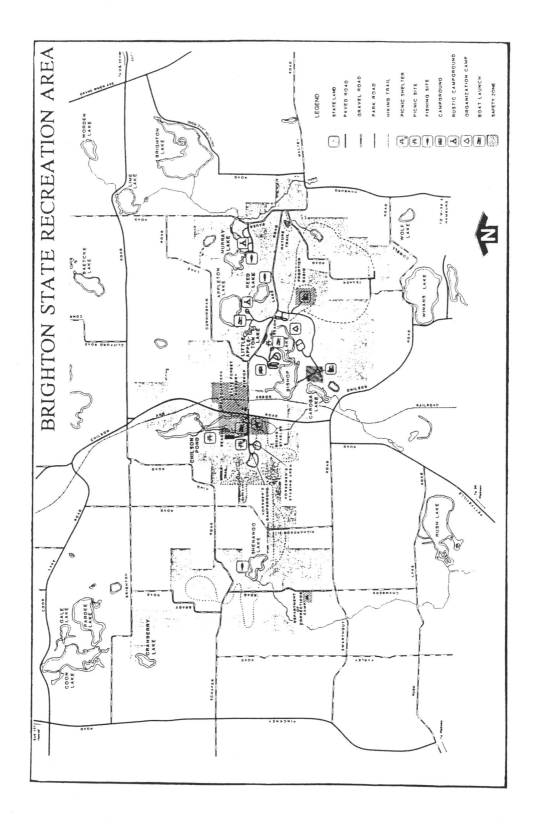

<table>
<tr><td>

7

</td><td>

DOUBLE JJ RESORT
PRIVATE
Oceana County - north of Muskegon

</td><td>

</td></tr>
</table>

The northern riding area of the 1,200 acre Double JJ Resort is over rolling dune ridges, through mature beech and maple woods, plantation pines, golf fairways and four lakes. Ride 6 miles to the west and you will be on the shore of Lake Michigan. The south trail is adjacent to a lake, pastures, hay fields and barns. This is where the resort has its breeding stock. This is a resort with many activities including a rodeo every Friday night during the season.

Note: You may bring your own horse with 1) a current health certificate (less than 30 days) and 2) current coggins (less than 6 months).

Horsemen's facilities:
Box stalls
Water
Bring your own grain/hay
Package deals for guests
26 miles of trails

For information:
Double JJ Resort   616-894-4444
PO Box 94
Routhbury, MI 49452

Fee

Directions: From Muskegon go north on 31 to the Routhbury Winston Rd. exit. Turn right (east) on Winston and go about 1 mile to Water Rd. (first road on the left). Turn left (north) and go 1 mile to the resort on the right. Turn in to office drive.

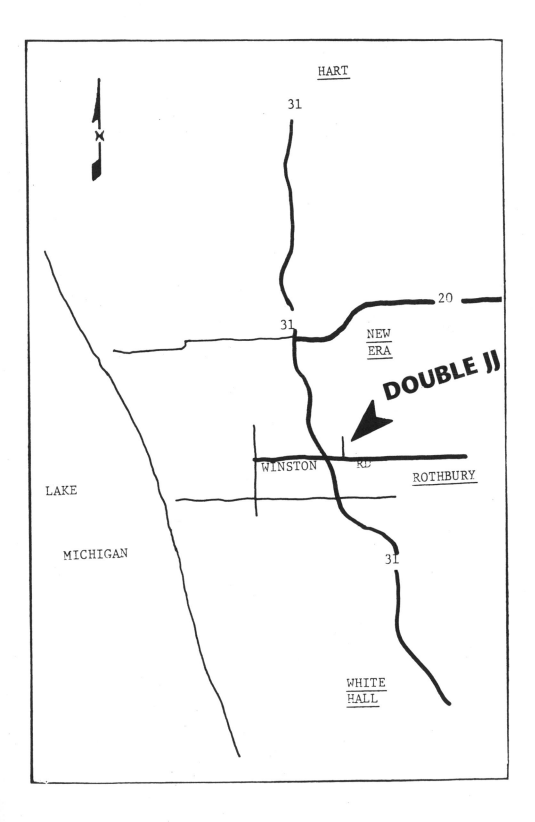

HART

31

20

31

NEW
ERA

DOUBLE JJ

WINSTON RD

ROTHBURY

LAKE

MICHIGAN

31

WHITE
HALL

8 ELBA EQUESTRIAN COMPLEX GENESEE COUNTY PARK
Genesse & Lapeer Counties - near Flint

Several lakes, a stream, fields, woods and wildlife are spread among rolling hills awaiting the rider in this secluded area of the 4,540 acre Genesse Recreation Area.

Note: Available for group camping by reservation only (minimum 10 days in advance). Call 810-736-7100.

Horsemen's facilities:
 Day use staging area
 20 rustic campsites
 Water
 Toilets
 Picket posts
 Miles of unmarked trails

For information:
 Genesse County Parks & Recreation Commission
 5045 Stanley Road
 Flint, MI 48506

Fee

Directions: The Elba Road exit is about 16 miles east of I-75. Go north on Elba Road about 6.5 miles and the complex is located on the left (west) side of the road.

Elba Equestrian Complex

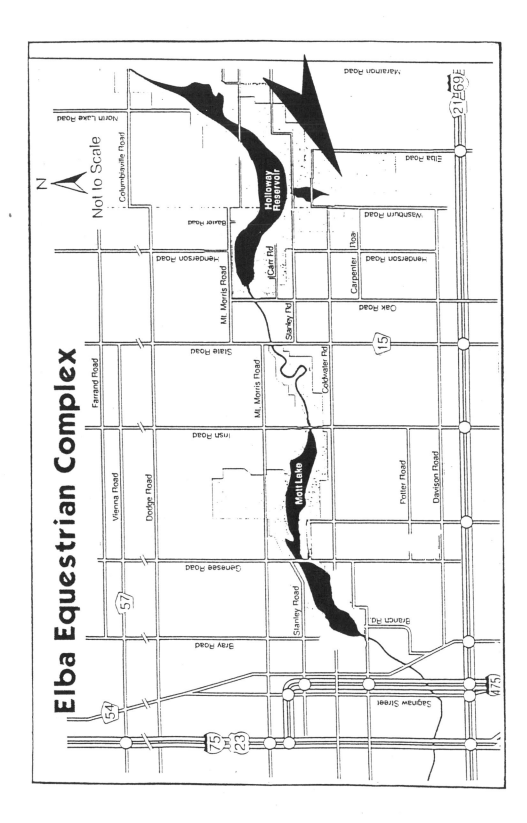

9 | EVERETT A. CUMMINGS CENTER GENESEE COUNTY PARK

Genesee County - northeast of Flint

The trails will take the rider through mature woods along the backwaters of Mott Lake and adjacent to the Flint River. The trails are not well-defined, but the area is open enough to find your way around. The land is mostly flat. Deer, beaver and small game are in the area of Cummings Center. In the spring, there are lots of wildflowers.

Horsemen's facilities:
Day use staging area Commission
Water (lake)
Toilets
Day trails (open dawn to sunset)

For information:
Genesee County Parks & Recreation
5045 Stanley Rd.
Flint, MI 48506
810-736-7100

No Fee

Directions: From I-75 exit at Mt. Morris Rd. (Exit 126) and go east about 10 miles to 6130 E. Mt. Morris Rd. (2 miles east of Genesee Rd.).

Everett A. Cummings Center

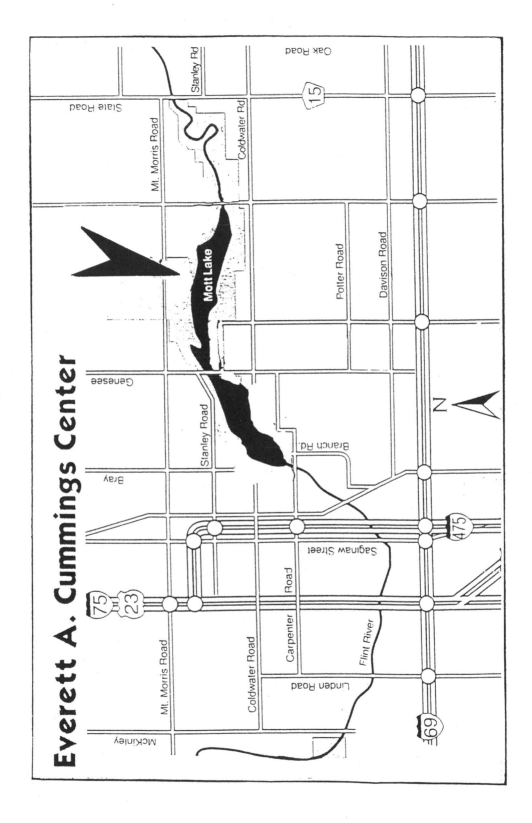

10	**FORT CUSTER** **RECREATION AREA** Kalamazoo County - west of Battle Creek	

The Fort Custer Recreation Area trails wind for 7 miles through wooded plains along fence lines, creeks, pine plantations, oak and what was farmland regrown with brush, scrub and young trees.

Horsemen's facilities:
Parking area at trailhead
7 miles of marked trails
Toilet

For information:
Fort Custer Recreation Area
5163 W. Fort Custer Drive
Augusta, MI 49012
616-731-4200

Fee

Directions: From I-94 exit at Mercury Road (Exit 92) and go north (Mercury Drive is also Business 94) about 4 miles to Dickman Road (M-96). Turn left and go about 4.5 miles to entrance on left (south) side of road. The Contact Station personnel will direct you to the staging and riding area.

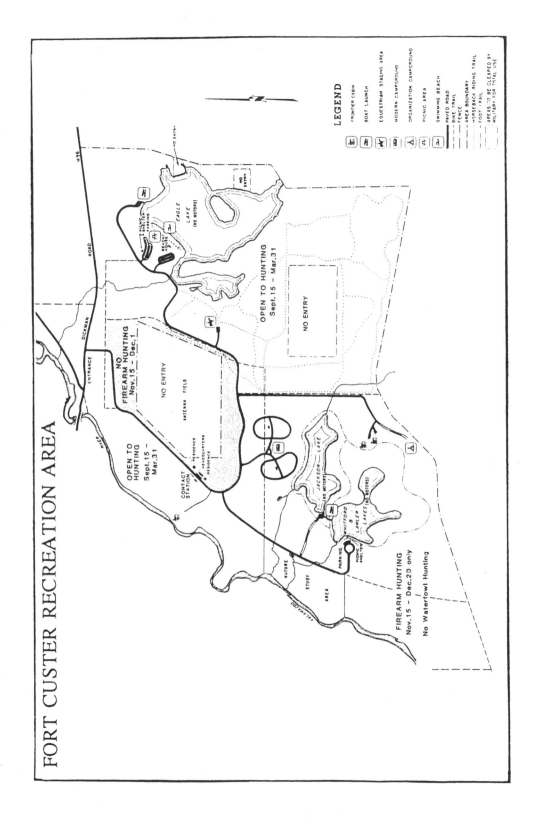

FORT CUSTER RECREATION AREA

LEGEND

🛖	FRONTIER CABIN
🚤	BOAT LAUNCH
🐎	EQUESTRIAN STAGING AREA
🚐	MODERN CAMPGROUND
⛺	ORGANIZATION CAMPGROUND
🛖	PICNIC AREA
🏊	SWIMMING BEACH

PAVED ROAD
BIKE TRAIL
FENCE
AREA BOUNDARY
HORSEBACK RIDING TRAIL
FOOT TRAIL
AREAS TO BE CLEARED BY MILITARY FOR TOTAL USE

OPEN TO HUNTING Sept.15 – Mar.31

NO FIREARM HUNTING Nov.15 – Dec.1

NO ENTRY

ANTENNA FIELD

OPEN TO HUNTING Sept. 15 – Mar.31

ENTRANCE

CONTACT STATION

RESIDENCE

HEADQUARTERS

RESIDENCE

EAGLE LAKE (NO MOTORS)

NO ENTRY

NO ENTRY

BEACH HOUSE

PICNIC SHELTER PARKING

DICKMAN ROAD

I-94

JACKSON LAKE (NO MOTORS)

WHITFORD & LAWLER LAKES (NO MOTORS)

PARKING

PICNIC SHELTER

NATURE STUDY AREA

FIREARM HUNTING Nov.15 – Dec.20 only

No Waterfowl Hunting

45

Highland Recreation Area is located in the rolling hills of southern Michigan encompassing 5,800 acres of forest, marshes and lakes. The trails offer panoramic vistas from some of the highest elevations in the region for the horsemen's enjoyment.

Horsemen's facilities:
Day use staging area
24 rustic campsites
Water
Toilets
Picket posts
13½ miles marked trails

For information:
Highland Recreation Area
5200 E Highland Road
Milford, MI 48042
810-685-2433

Fee

Directions: From US 23 exit at Highland Road - M-59 (Exit 67). Travel east about 10.5 miles to the Highland Recreation Area entrance located on the right (south) side of the road. From I-75 exit at M-59 (Exit 77) and travel west about 16.5 miles and the entrance will be on the left. You must stop inside the park to pay fees and there you will receive an area map.

HIGHLAND RECREATION AREA

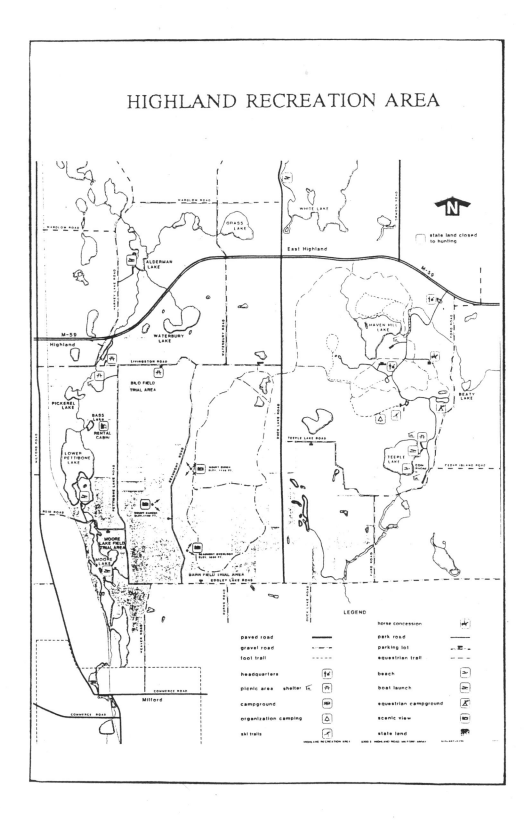

| 12 | **HUNGERFORD LAKE**
MANISTEE NATIONAL FOREST
Newaygo County - west of Big Rapids |  |

Hungerford Lake Recreation Area is a multiple-use area and is popular with trail riders. The horseman has an opportunity to ride dirt single tracks that meander through the woods up and down hills and down along Hungerford Lake. There are also miles of two-tracks that traverse this part of the Manistee National Forest.

Horsemen's facilities:
Rustic camp area
13 miles of marked cross country ski trails
Miles of two-tracks

For information:
Manistee National Forest
District Ranger
12 N. Charles St.
White Cloud, MI 49349
616-689-6696
800-821-6263

No fee

Directions: From US 131 and M-20 near Big Rapids (Exit 139) go west about 5 miles (where M-20 turns south) to Cypress Ave. and go right (north). Go .5 mile to stop sign and turn right (east) on Hungerford Lake Rd. Go about .5 mile to the stop sign at the "T". Turn left (north) on to the dirt road (No. 5134) and go about 1.1 miles to a two-track on the right. It is a short two-track to a rustic camping area.

Hungerford Lake Recreation Area

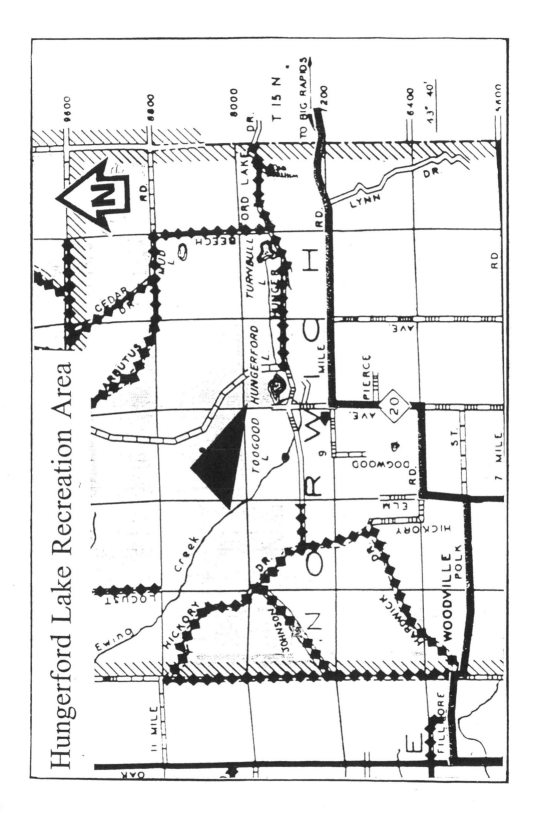

IONIA RECREATION AREA

13

Ionia County - southwest of Ionia

Twenty miles of horse trails loop through the southern half of this 4,085 acre park. These well-marked trails will take the rider over rolling hills with scenic views around open meadows, into deep woods, open fields and across small streams. This parks habitat supports many wildflowers, a large variety of birds, including heron, which may be seen when riding adjacent to the wild side of the lake. Wildlife includes fox, deer and quail.

Horsemen's facilities:
Day use staging area
49 rustic campsites with picnic tables
Water
Shower facilities (April- Sept.)
Toilets
Picket posts
20 miles of marked trails
Group camp available (5 camps or more to reserve)

For information:
Ionia Recreation Area
2880 David Highway
Ionia, MI 48846
616-527-3750

Fee

Directions: From I-96 exit Jordan Lake road (Exit 64) and go north about 3.5 miles to the park entrance.

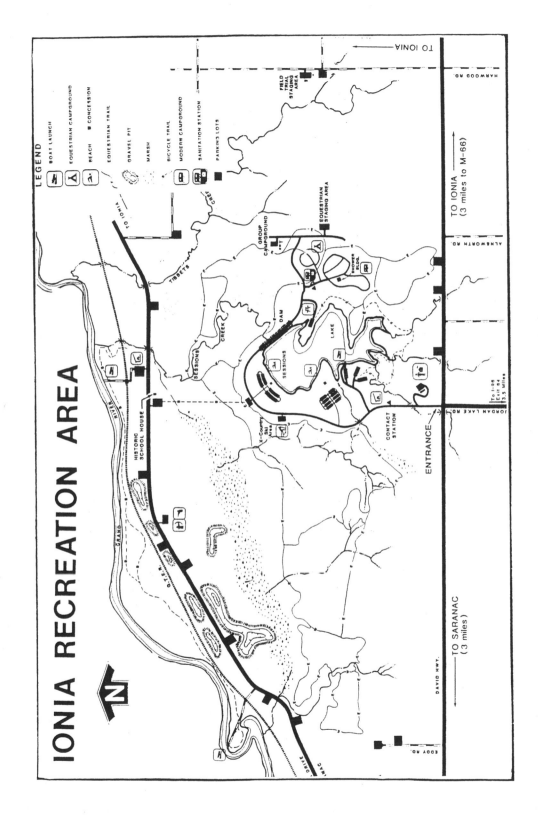

IONIA RECREATION AREA

LEGEND

♨	BOAT LAUNCH
⛺	EQUESTRIAN CAMPGROUND
⛱	BEACH ■ CONCESSION
	EQUESTRIAN TRAIL
	GRAVEL PIT
	MARSH
	BICYCLE TRAIL
🚻	MODERN CAMPGROUND
🚻	SANITATION STATION
■	PARKING LOTS

51

The trail is a 34-mile hiking trail from Kalamazoo to South Haven with the horse trail running parallel to it for 14 miles, from 2 miles east of South Haven to Bloomingdale. The trails are separated for most of the lengths by a variety of trees and bushes as it winds east and west. Hitching rails have been installed at locations along the path and riders can bring buckets to water their horses.

Park rules & guidelines: Trail hours are 8AM to 10PM; tie horses away from trees; no riding on limestone path; on the main trail, keep to the outer edge; yield to bikers and hikers; stop at intersections.

Note: Trail pass is required for all and are available at the east and west trailheads, Van Buren State Park, trail ranger and any business displaying the trail logo.

Horsemen's facilities:
    Staging (parking)
        in Kibbie (CR 687)
        in Lacota (CR 681)
        in Bloomingdale (CR 665)
    Water at parking areas
    Toilets on trail

For information:
    Van Buren State Park
    23960 Ruggles Road
    South Haven, MI 49090
    616-637-2788

Fee

Directions: The west staging area can be reached from I-196 and CR 388 (Exit 20). Go east about 3.25 miles to CR 687 (68th St.) and go north about 1 mile to trailhead on the left.

Kal-Haven Trail Sesquicentennial State Park

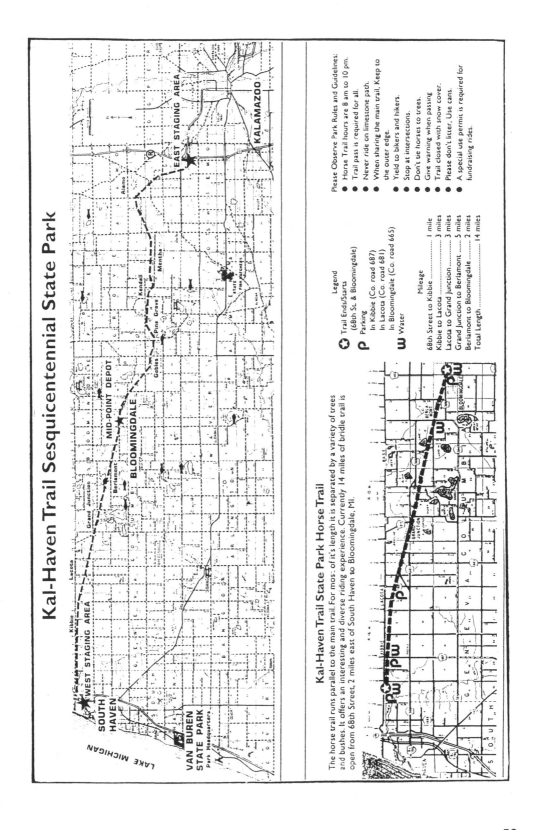

Kal-Haven Trail State Park Horse Trail

The horse trail runs parallel to the main trail. For most of it's length it is separated by a variety of trees and bushes. It offers an interesting and diverse riding experience. Currently 14 miles of bridle trail is open from 68th Street, 2 miles east of South Haven to Bloomingdale, MI.

Legend

⭐ Trail Ends/Starts
(68th St. & Bloomingdale)

P Parking
In Kibbie (Co. road 687)
In Lacota (Co. road 681)
In Bloomingdale (Co. road 665)

w Water

Mileage

68th Street to Kibbie	1 mile
Kibbie to Lacota	3 miles
Lacota to Grand Junction	3 miles
Grand Junction to Berlamont	5 miles
Berlamont to Bloomingdale	2 miles
Total Length	14 miles

Please Observe Park Rules and Guidelines:

- Horse Trail hours are 8 am to 10 pm.
- Trail pass is required for all.
- Never ride on limestone path.
- When sharing the main trail, Keep to the outer edge.
- Yield to bikers and hikers.
- Stop at intersections.
- Don't tie horses to trees.
- Give warning when passing
- Trail closed with snow cover.
- Please don't litter. Use cans.
- A special use permit is required for fundraising rides.

53

	KENSINGTON METROPARK	
15	Oakland and Livingston Counties East of Brighton; west of Wixom	

Kensington Metropark is located in western Oakland County, comprised of 5,000 acres and encompasses Kent Lake. The trail ambles through hardwoods, fields and low rolling hills among the western side of the park.

Horsemen's facilities:
Day use staging area
Horse entrance off Buno Rd.
8.5 miles of marked trail

For information:
Kensington Metropark
2240 W. Buno Rd.
Milford, MI 493880
810-685-1561 or 800-47-PARKS

Directions: Exit I-96 via Kent Lake Rd. (Exit 153) and turn north on Huron River Parkway (to sign release and purchase riding tag) on Buno Rd. Watch for signs.

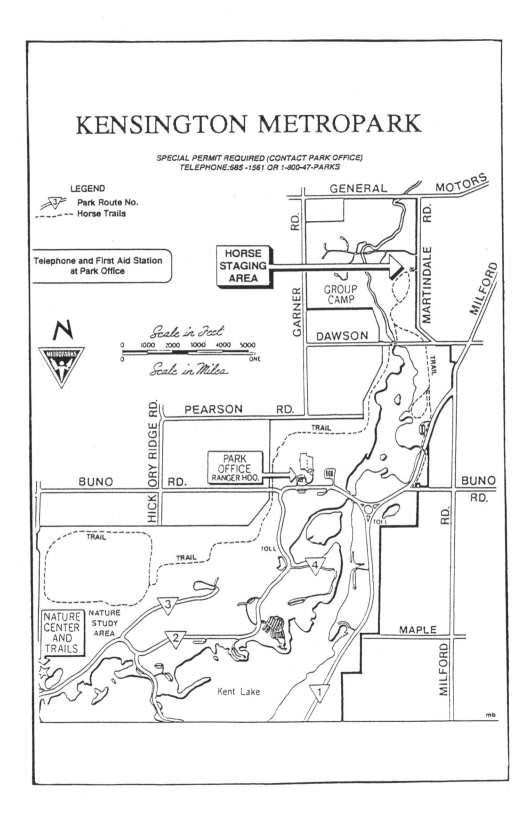

KENSINGTON METROPARK

SPECIAL PERMIT REQUIRED (CONTACT PARK OFFICE)
TELEPHONE:685-1561 OR 1-800-47-PARKS

LEGEND
Park Route No.
Horse Trails

Telephone and First Aid Station
at Park Office

N
METROPARKS

Scale in Feet
0   1000 2000 3000 4000 5000
0   ONE
Scale in Miles

GENERAL MOTORS

HORSE STAGING AREA

GROUP CAMP

GARNER RD.

MARTINDALE RD.

MILFORD

DAWSON

TRAIL

PEARSON RD.

TRAIL

PARK OFFICE
RANGER HDO.

HICKORY RIDGE RD.

BUNO RD.

BUNO RD.

TOLL

TRAIL

TRAIL

TOLL

4

3

2

NATURE CENTER AND TRAILS

NATURE STUDY AREA

MAPLE

MILFORD

RD.

1

Kent Lake

mb

55

16 KINROSS RV PARK WEST

Chippewa County - north of Mackinac Bridge

The terrain in this area of northern Michigan is as varied as the weather. The trail you choose to ride will determine whether you go through the state lands or national forests. The terrain may encompass flats, rolling hills, rocky trails, hardwoods and small streams. Many of the trails open to a scenic view.

Horsemen's facilities:
 52 modern campsites
 Water
 Electricity
 Toilets
 Dump station
 Shower facilities
 Horse stalls
 Riding arena - pre-scheduling necessary
 Group camping area with advance notice
 Unmarked trails - maps available of area

For information:
 Kinross Park and Recreation
 PO Box 175
 Kinross, MI 49752
 906-495-5381

Fee

Directions: Leave I-75 at Exit 378 and travel east about .5 miles on Tone Rd. to county fairgrounds. Turn left into RV Park West.

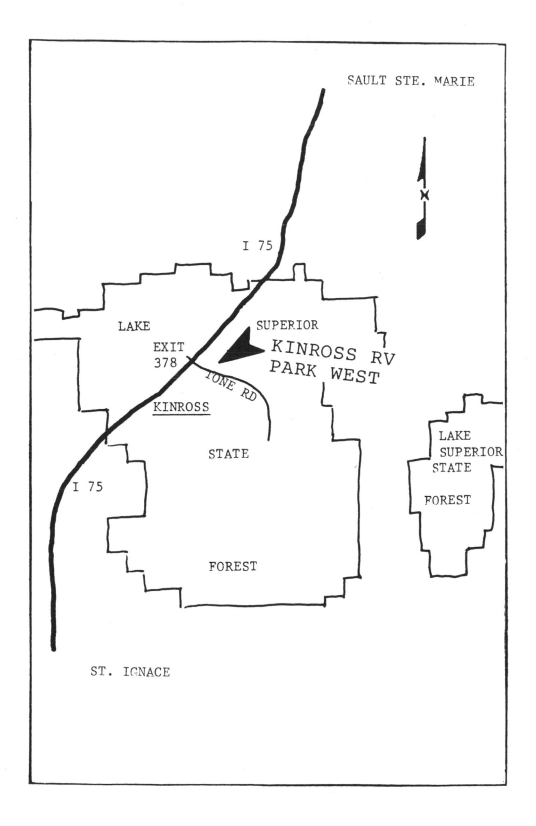

17 LAKELANDS TRAIL STATE PARK
Ingham and Livingston Counties

Lake Trail from Pinckney to Stockbridge: This trail was opened the summer of 1994. There is riding on grass along open fields, wetlands and farm fields through hardwood over several short bridges along the old railroad bed. Depending on the time and how tranquil the day, you may see deer, waterfowl or other types of wildlife.

Horsemen's facilities:
    Pinckney trailhead (east)
    Stockbridge (west)
    Water
    Toilet
    13-14 miles of horse trail parallel with compacted slag walking trail

For information:
    Pinckney Recreation Area
    RR 1, 8555 Silver Lake Rd.
    Pinckney, MI 48169
    313-426-4913

Fee: State park trail pass needed; available at Pinckney Recreation Area and many local businesses.

Directions: East trailhead is located on M-19 4 blocks north of M-36 in the Village of Pinckney on the west side of M-19. The west trailhead is located in the City of Stockbridge, 7 blocks south of where M-52 and M-106 split and go east and west. The trailhead is locate on the east side of M-52 and M-106.

LAKELANDS TRAIL STATE PARK

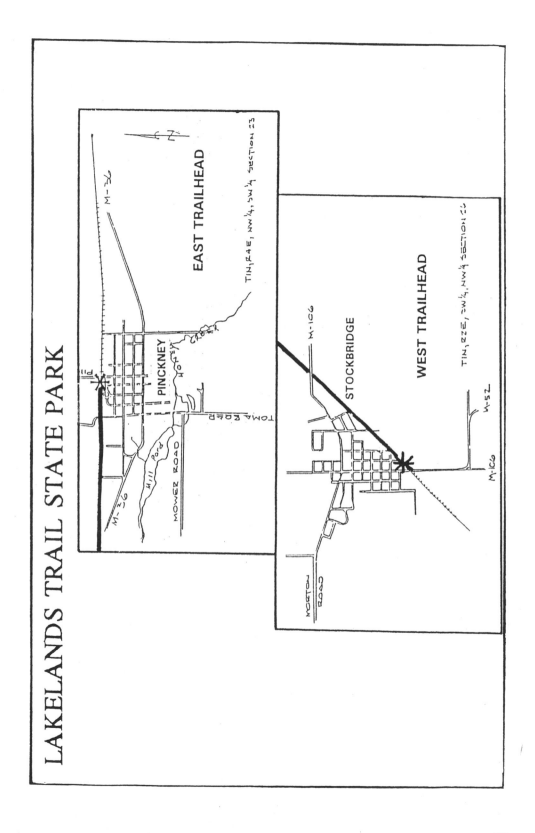

MAYBURY STATE PARK
18
Wayne County - west of Northville

Maybury State park contains almost 1,000 acres of gently rolling terrain, open meadows, mature forest, and variety of wildlife and abundant wildflowers, all for the horseman's enjoyment.

Horsemen's facilities:
   Day use staging area off Beck Rd.
   Toilets
   Water
   11 miles of marked trails
   Ride-in off 8 Mile Road
   Riding stable off Beck Road: 810-347-1088

For information:
   Maybury State Park
   20145 Beck Road
   Northville, MI 48167
   810-349-8390

Fee

Directions: From I-25 exit at 8 Mile Road (Exit 167) go about five miles west on 8 Mile Road to Beck Road. Turn left (south) about .25 mile on right into horseman's entrance and staging area. From M-14 exit at Beck Road (Exit 18) and go north on Beck Rd.. about 3.5 miles to horsemen's entrance and staging area.

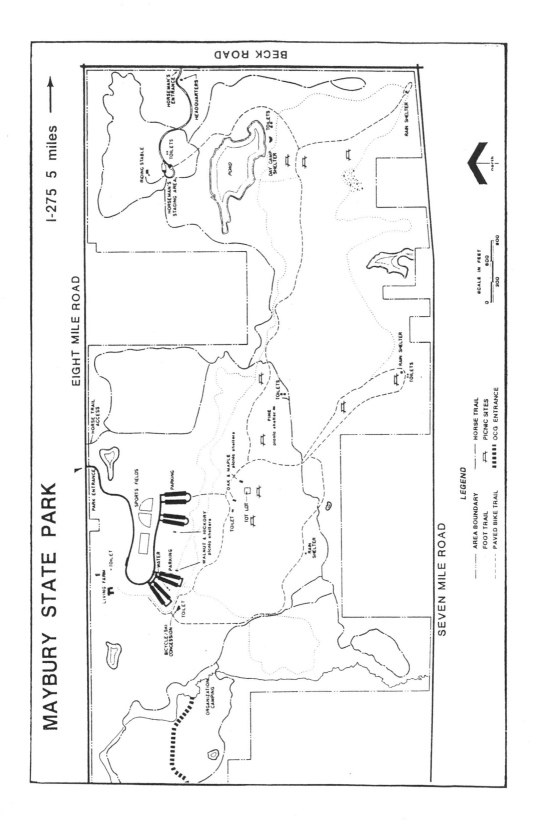

MAYBURY STATE PARK

I-275 5 miles →

EIGHT MILE ROAD

SEVEN MILE ROAD

BECK ROAD

LEGEND

—·—·— AREA BOUNDARY

———— FOOT TRAIL

– – – – PAVED BIKE TRAIL

········· HORSE TRAIL

⚑ PICNIC SITES

▪▪▪▪▪ OCG ENTRANCE

SCALE IN FEET

0   200   600   800

north

PARK ENTRANCE

LIVING FARM

TOILET

SPORTS FIELDS

PARKING

WATER

PARKING

WALNUT & HICKORY picnic shelters

BICYCLE/SKI CONCESSION

TOILET

ORGANIZATION CAMPING

HORSE TRAIL ACCESS

OAK & MAPLE picnic shelters

TOILET

TOT LOT

PINE picnic shelters

TOILETS

RAW SHELTER

RAW SHELTER

TOILETS

HORSEMAN'S ENTRANCE

HEADQUARTERS

RIDING STABLE

TOILETS

HORSEMAN'S STAGING AREA

POND

TOILETS

DAY CAMP SHELTER

RAW SHELTER

19 ORTONVILLE RECREATION AREA (HADLEY HILLS)

Lapeer and Oakland Counties - northwest of Oxford;
northeast of Holly

The horseman will ride trails over the highest hills in Lapeer County that offer the finest views of the region. The trails pass around several of the parks small lakes, ponds and marshlands. In season there are many flowering trees and wildflowers. The rider may see wildlife both large and small.

Horsemen's facilities:
Day use staging area
Rustic campsites with picnic tables
Water
Toilets
17 miles of marked and unmarked trails

For information:
Ortonville Recreation Area
RR 2, 5767 Hadley Rd..
Ortonville, MI 48462
810-797-4439

Fee

Directions: From I-75 and M-15 (Exit 91) go north to Goodrich and turn right on Hegle Road. From I-69 and M-15 (Exit 145) go south to Goodrich and turn left on Hegle Road. Go about 5.5 miles on Hegle Rd.. to Hadley Rd.. Turn right (south) and go about 1.5 miles to Fox Rd.. Turn right (west) and go about .75 miles to the camp on the right. Watch for sign.

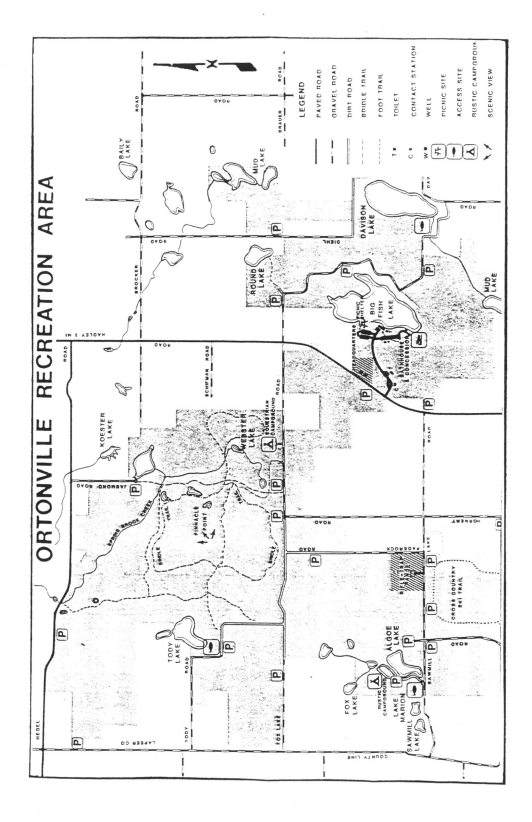

ORTONVILLE RECREATION AREA

LEGEND

PAVED ROAD	
GRAVEL ROAD	
DIRT ROAD	
BRIDLE TRAIL	
FOOT TRAIL	
TOILET	T
CONTACT STATION	C
WELL	W
PICNIC SITE	
ACCESS SITE	
RUSTIC CAMPGROUND	
SCENIC VIEW	

63

The Paint Creek Trail is a pleasant 6 mile flat ride along the meandering Paint Creek through aspen growth, meadows and scenic rolling hills. You can enjoy a quiet look at nature along the trail.

Horsemen's facilities:
　　6 miles of trail for horses
　　Staging areas:
　　　　Clarkson Rd..
　　　　Gallagher Rd..
　　Cider mill close by
　　Not allowed to trot or canter on limestone; use grassy areas

For information:
　　Paint Creek Trailway Commission
　　4393 Collins Rd..
　　Rochester, MI 48306
　　810-651-9260

Directions: From Rochester go north on Orion Rd.. to Gallagher Rd.. about 3 miles (next to cider mill). Turn left and go over bridge. Turn right in to parking lot for staging.

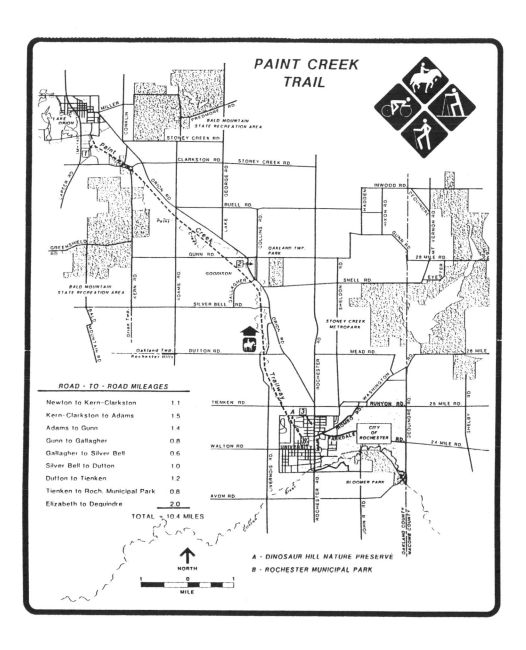

PAINT CREEK TRAIL

ROAD - TO - ROAD MILEAGES

Newton to Kern-Clarkston	1.1
Kern-Clarkston to Adams	1.5
Adams to Gunn	1.4
Gunn to Gallagher	0.8
Gallagher to Silver Bell	0.6
Silver Bell to Dutton	1.0
Dutton to Tienken	1.2
Tienken to Roch. Municipal Park	0.8
Elizabeth to Dequindre	2.0
TOTAL = 10.4 MILES	

NORTH

|———|———|———|
1   0   1
MILE

A - DINOSAUR HILL NATURE PRESERVE
B - ROCHESTER MUNICIPAL PARK

65

PINCKNEY RECREATION AREA

21

Washtenaw & Livingston Counties - near Pinckney

The Pinckney Recreation Area's riding trails are located in the northern most portion of this 11,000 acre recreation area. The trails will take the rider through oak, pine, maple and dogwood, over rolling hills to lookout hill where the entire countryside comes into view, including Peach Mountain Observatory. Deer, fox, ground hogs and other small game abound in this area.

Horsemen's facilities:
Day use staging area
Toilets
Water
8 miles of unmarked trails
Riding stables (313-878-3632)

For information:
Pinckney Recreation Area
RR 1, 8555 Silver Hill Rd..
Pinckney, MI 48169
313-426-4913

Fee

Directions: From D-19 and M-36 in Pinckney go about 1.5 miles west to Cedar Lake Rd.. and turn left (south) about 1 mile to Monks Rd.. Turn right (west) and go about 1 mile to the staging area on the left side of the road.

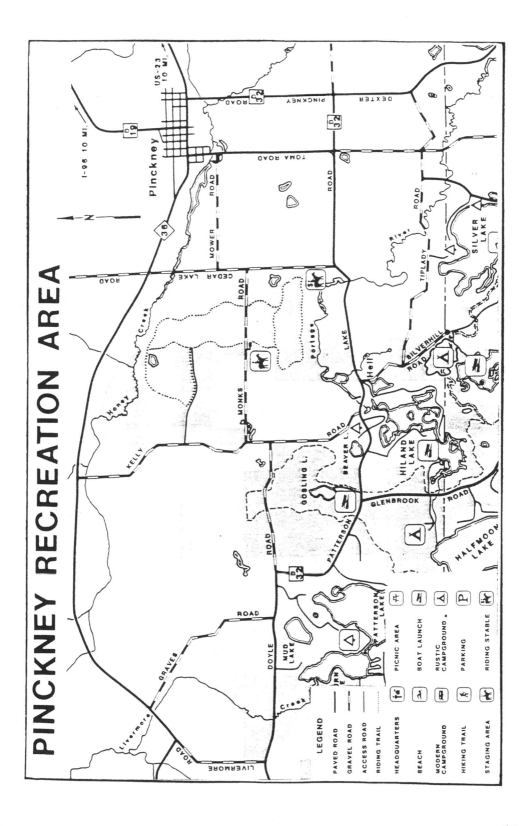

PINCKNEY RECREATION AREA

LEGEND

——	PAVED ROAD
——	GRAVEL ROAD
——	ACCESS ROAD
····	RIDING TRAIL

HEADQUARTERS

BEACH

MODERN CAMPGROUND

HIKING TRAIL

STAGING AREA

PICNIC AREA

BOAT LAUNCH

RUSTIC CAMPGROUND

PARKING

RIDING STABLE

67

22 | PINE MARTIN RUN TRAIL
Schoolcraft County - northwest of Manistique
in the Hiawatha National Forest

Pine Martin Run is a 26-mile system of five loop trails with interconnecting spurs located in the Ironjaw Semi-Primitive Area. This trail crosses through a grouse management area, traverses rolling hills of beech, birch and maple as it winds around lakes and level terrain of pine plantations interspersed with hardwoods and hemlocks. The trail loops through a variety of vegetation, topography, plant communities, offering many wildlife viewing opportunities.

Trail segments: Rumble Lake, 4.3 miles; Swan Lake, 3.8 miles; Ironjaw Lake, 4.6 miles; Spud Lake, 6.4 miles; Triangle Lake, 7.2 miles

Trail notes: Be prepared for insects and please 1) pack in, pack out, 2) Picket your horse at least 100 Feet from lakes and streams, 3) dismantle temporary hitch rails and scatter manure, 4) be cautious and courteous - this is a multi-use trail.

Horsemen's facilities:
Trailhead parking - rustic campsites
Water & toilets (CR 440 trailhead)
Toilets only (other trailheads)
Adirondak shelters
Fire rings (Rim Lake, Rumble Lake, and along Indian River)

For information:
Hiawatha National Forest
Manistique Ranger District
Manistique, MI 49843
906-341-5666

Directions: From Manistique go west on US 2 about 10.5 miles to CR 437 (Cooks School Rd..). Turn right (north) and go about 18 miles to CR 440. Turn left (west) about 1 mile to the CR 440 trailhead where you will find parking, water and toilets.

Pine Marten Run Trail

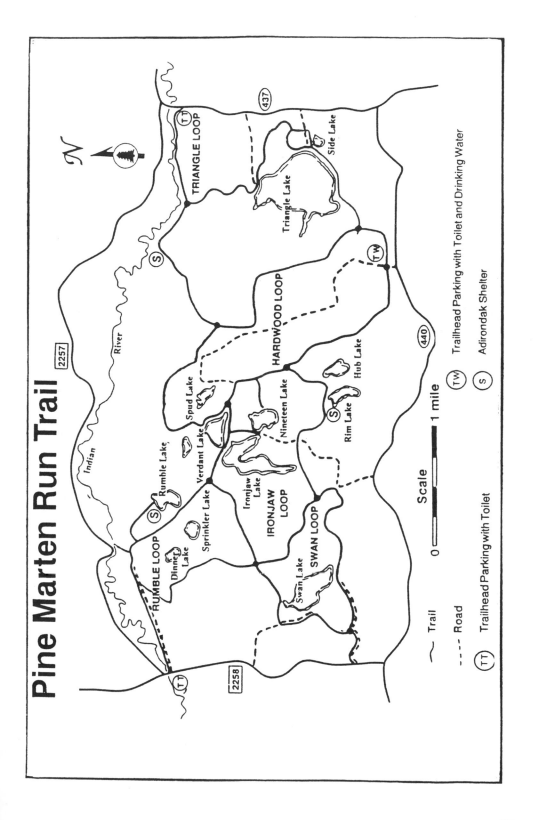

	PONTIAC LAKE
23	**RECREATION AREA** Oakland County

Horse trails cut through the entire park and include riding along the Huron River and rising up to some very scenic overlooks. One can view a variety of wildlife, wildflowers and ecosystems.

Horsemen's facilities:
Day use staging area
25 rustic campsites
Toilets
Water
17 miles of marked horse trails shared with mountain bikers
Public riding stables 810-685-2433

For information:
Pontiac Lake Recreation Area
7800 Gale Rd..
Waterford, MI 48327
810-666-1020

Fee

Directions: The way into Pontiac Lake Horse Camp is from Teggerdine Rd.. Teggerdine Rd.. runs north from M-59 about 14 miles east of US-23 and about 9.25 miles west of Telegraph (US-24). Take Teggerdine north about 2.5 miles to the camp road on the right (area sign on left). Drive about 2 miles in to the camp on the right.

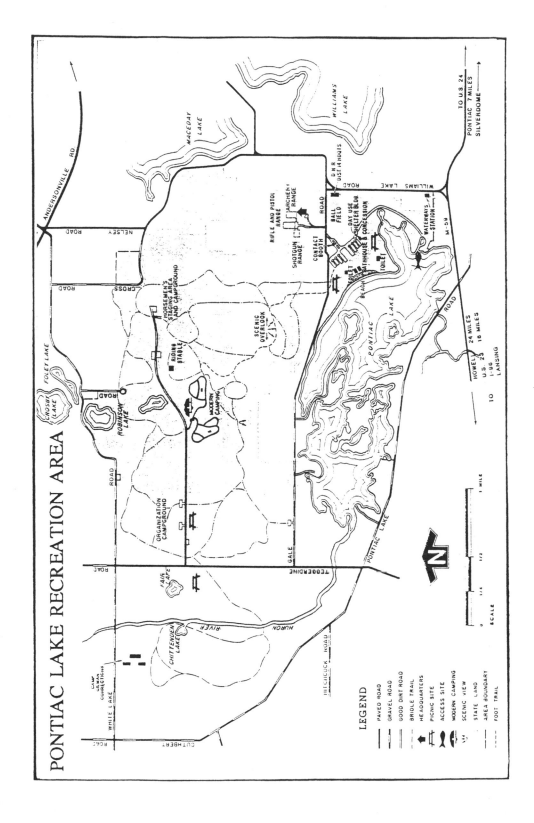

PONTIAC LAKE RECREATION AREA

LEGEND

	PAVED ROAD
	GRAVEL ROAD
	GOOD DIRT ROAD
	BRIDLE TRAIL
	HEADQUARTERS
	PICNIC SITE
	ACCESS SITE
	MODERN CAMPING
	SCENIC VIEW
	STATE LAND
	AREA BOUNDARY
	FOOT TRAIL

N

SCALE

0   1/4   1/2   1 MILE

71

PROUD LAKE RECREATION AREA

24 Oakland County - southeast of Milford

The trails of Proud Lake Recreation Area will take the rider across flatlands, over low rising hills and meadows, and through red and white pine, oak, maple, elm and beech woods. There are lots of birds and small wildlife. In the spring the lowlands retain water with the result being an abundance of wildflowers.

Horsemen's facilities:
Day use staging area
Toilet
8 miles of marked trails shared with mountain bikers

For information:
Proud Lake Recreation Area
R 3, 3540 Wixom Rd..
Milford, MI 48382
810-685-2433

Fee

Directions: From the Milford Rd. exit on I-96 (Exit 155) travel north about 2.5 miles to Buno Rd.. Turn right (east) and go about 2.5 miles to Childs Lake Rd. and turn left (north) to the Proud Lake Recreation Staging Area.

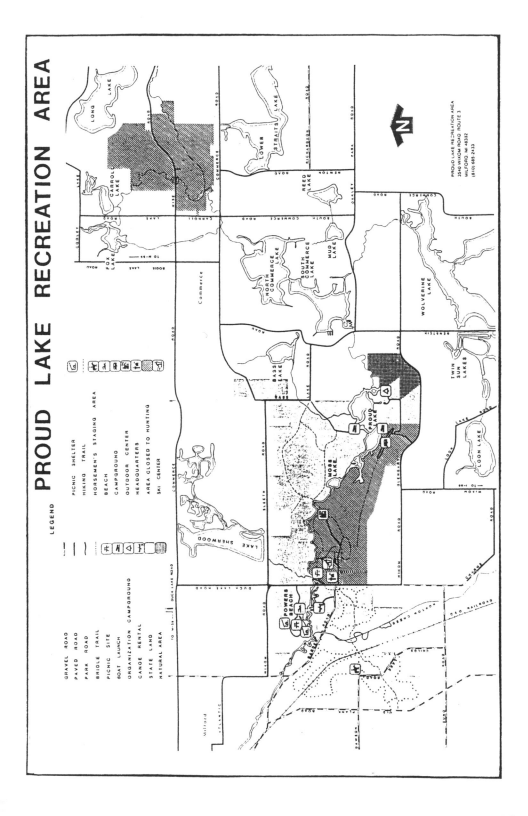

PROUD LAKE RECREATION AREA

You can go northeast of southwest on the Shore-to-Shore Trail exploring terrain, vegetation, colors and wildlife, including rolling, sandy hills with pine, beech, aspen and oak trees, or ridges overlooking the Boardman River. There are horse trails, snowmobile trails and two-tracks. Ranch Rudolf is located .5 miles north of Scheck's Trail Camp.

Note: Horse camping May-June, September-October by reservation only.

Horsemen's facilities:
　　Modern campsites
　　Toilets
　　Water
　　Showers
　　Restaurant
　　Fire pit
　　Maximum 4 people, 2 horses per site

For information:
　　Ranch Rudolf
　　6841 Brown Bridge Rd..
　　Traverse City, MI 49686
　　616-947-9529

Fee

Directions: From the east - On Highway 131 the blinking yellow light in South Boardman turn west (coming from Kalkaska, about 8 miles turn right) (coming from Cadillac, about 28 miles turn left). Travel west on Boardman Rd.. and Supply Rd.., about 6 miles to Brown Bridge Rd.. Turn left (south) and go about 3 miles to the entrance of Ranch Rudolf on the right. Watch for signs. From the west - via Highway 37 and Highway 31 (Chums Corner) go east on Beitner Rd.. about 1.6 miles to River Rd.. and turn right. Follow River Rd.. about 6.5 miles and it will become Brown Bridge Rd.. Continue straight and Ranch Rudolf will be about 4.25 miles on your left next to the Boardman River. Watch for signs.

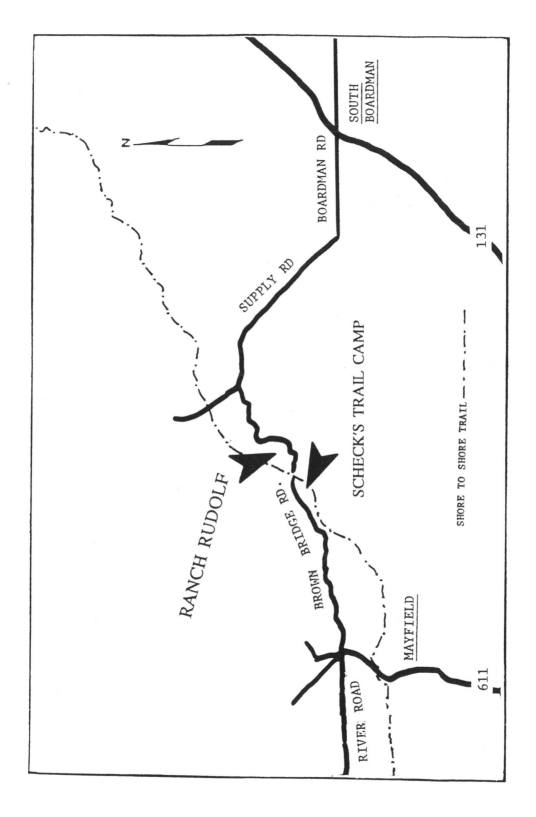

26 | ROSE LAKE WILDLIFE RESEARCH AREA

Clinton & Shiawasse Counties - northeast of Lansing

Rose Lake is comprised of 3,646 acres of moderately rolling farmland, abandoned fields, oak and lowland woods and marsh divided into 7 color designated areas for research purposes. The wildlife management areas feature ponds, flooding, brush piles, food patches, trees and shrub plantings), soil conservation practices, wildlife research and a pathology laboratory.

Trail notes: The work roads are the trail. Riders are not to take horses off the roads or ride in a group larger than 3 horses.

Horsemen's facilities
>   Day use parking lot
>   Water
>   Restroom in office

For information:
>   Rose Lake Wildlife Research Center
>   8562 E. Stoll Rd..
>   E. Lansing, MI 48823

No fee

Directions: From I-69 take Exit 94. Go the to light and turn left to old M-78. Go about .5 miles then turn left on Upton Rd.. Go 1.5 miles and turn right on Stoll Rd.. The office is .25 miles on right. Maps are available at the office.

ROSE LAKE WILDLIFE RESEARCH AREA

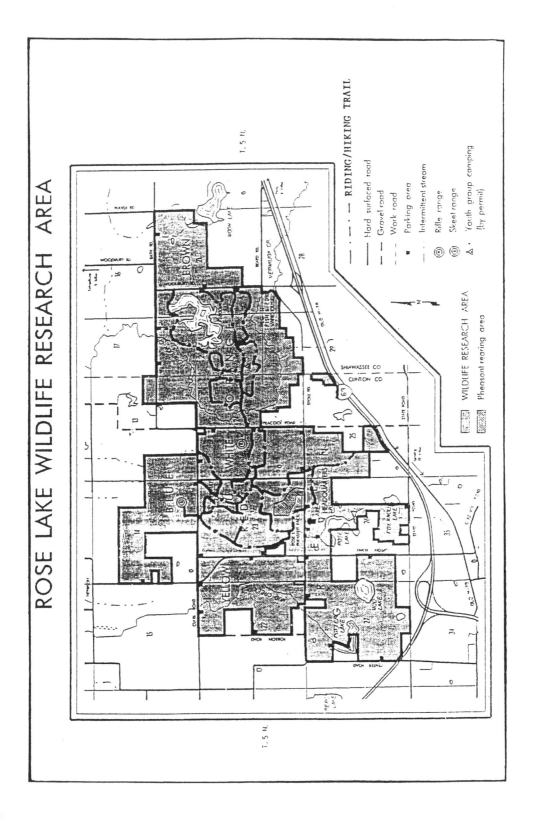

27 SLEEPING BEAR DUNES NATIONAL LAKESHORE ALLIGATOR HILL HIKING TRAIL

Leelanau County - northwest of Traverse City; north of Empire

You can spend a day riding in this area visiting the Sleeping Bear Dunes National Lakeshore and explore the sand dunes of Alligator Hill Hiking Trail and see the crystal blue waters of Glen Lake and Lake Michigan.

Horsemen's facilities:
Trailhead parking lot is staging area
Toilets
8 miles of marked trails

For information:
Sleeping Bear Dunes National Lakeshore
9922 Front St.
Empire, MI 49630
616-326-5134

Directions: From Empire travel north on State Highway 22 about 2 miles to Highway 109. Turn left (north) for about 4 miles to Day Forest Rd.. to Stocking Rd.. and the trailhead.

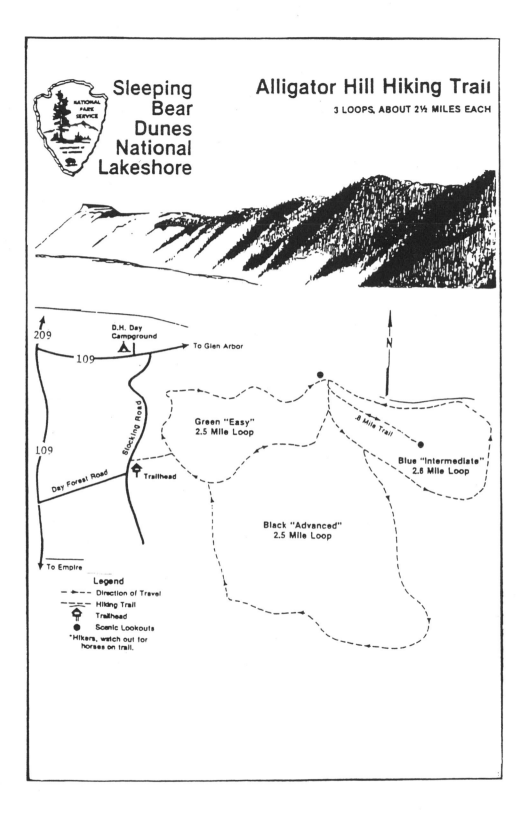

Sleeping Bear Dunes National Lakeshore

Alligator Hill Hiking Trail
3 LOOPS, ABOUT 2½ MILES EACH

209
109
D.H. Day Campground
To Glen Arbor
Stocking Road
109
Day Forest Road
Trailhead
To Empire

N

.8 Mile Trail

Green "Easy" 2.5 Mile Loop

Blue "Intermediate" 2.6 Mile Loop

Black "Advanced" 2.5 Mile Loop

Legend
- Direction of Travel
- Hiking Trail
- Trailhead
- Scenic Lookouts

*Hikers, watch out for horses on trail.

28 THE NORDHOUSE DUNES WILDERNESS
MANISTEE NATIONAL FOREST
Mason County - North of Ludington

The Nordhouse Dunes area was designated a wilderness by the 1987 Michigan Wilderness Act. It is the only federally designated wilderness in the Lower Peninsula and encompasses 3,450 acres of the Manistee National Forest. The unique ecology of the wilderness includes 3 miles of beach, active and forested dunes, inter-dunal wetlands, a forested lake bed and marsh.

Please practice no-trace camping.

Horsemen's facilities:
    Rustic camping

For information:
    Manistee Ranger District
    1658 Manistee Highway
    Manistee, MI 49660
    616-723-2211

Directions: From US 31 go west on Forest Trail about 2.5 miles to Quarterline Rd. Then south about 1.5 miles on Quarterline to Nurnberg Rd. Then left (west) about 6 miles to the large parking/camping area at the end of the road.

THE NORDHOUSE DUNES WILDERNESS

NORDHOUSE DUNES WILDERNESS REGULATIONS

We need your help in order to maintain the unique qualities of the wilderness. Your cooperation is the key to protecting this special area for future generations.

• Group size of *ten* or fewer people.

• Mechanical and motorized vehicles and equipment are not permitted. This includes *bike* and wheeled carts. (motorized wheelchairs are an exception)

• Campfires and campsites must be more than 400 feet from Lake Michigan, and wilderness boundaries; 200 feet from Nordhouse Lake. *NO BEACH FIRES!*

• Public nudity is not allowed.

• Driftwood must not be removed from the wilderness or burned.

LEGEND

⌒⌒	Trails
·⌒·⌒·	Wilderness Boundary
⋮⋮⋮	Non-wilderness Areas
═══	Dirt road
═══	Good dirt road
───	Paved road
⋏⋏⋏	Swamps
	Dune Areas

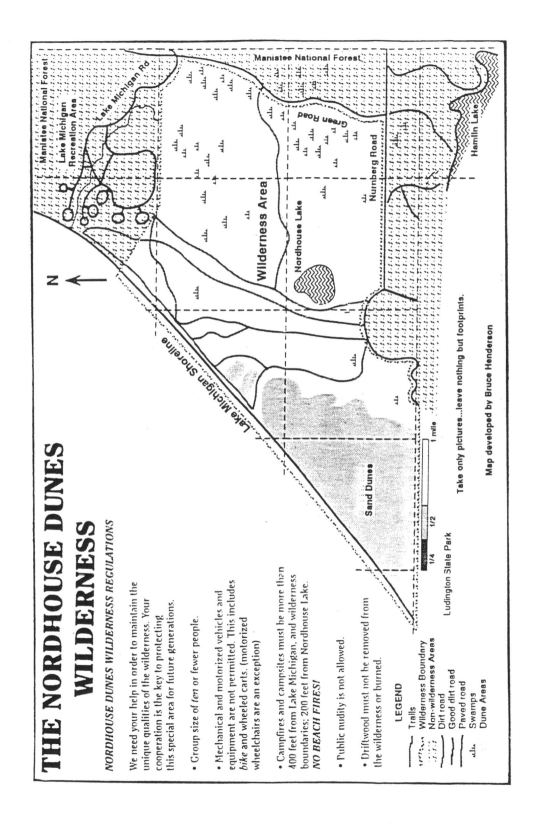

Manistee National Forest

Lake Michigan Rd

Lake Michigan Recreation Area

Manistee National Forest

Green Road

Nurnberg Road

Hamlin Lake

Wilderness Area

Nordhouse Lake

Lake Michigan Shoreline

N ←

Sand Dunes

Ludington State Park

1/4   1/2   1 mile

Take only pictures...leave nothing but footprints.

Map developed by Bruce Henderson

29	**THOMPSON'S HARBOR** **STATE PARK** Presque Isle County - southeast of Rogers City	

This Michigan State Park of 5,200 acres is basically undeveloped. Currently there are 6.4 miles of trails that loop through a low-hilled section of the park. Loop Three will take the rider to the limestone shore of Lake Huron. Along the lake the terrain is low and marshy and has an open desert-like appearance with its sand and grass formations - then it's back into the woods. The park also has terrain of cobblestone and limestone.

Horsemen's facilities:
   Day use parking area at trailhead
   Water for horses (Lake Huron)
   6.4 miles of marked trails
   Three loops shared with hikers

For information:
   Hoeft State Park
   US 23 North
   Rogers City, MI 49799
   517-734-2543

No fee

Directions: On US 23 about 13 miles south of Rogers City on the left (north) side of the highway pull into the park. In about 1.5 miles the road will fork. Take the right road about 2 miles to a parking lot. This area is used as a staging area and trailhead.

THOMPSON'S HARBOR STATE PARK

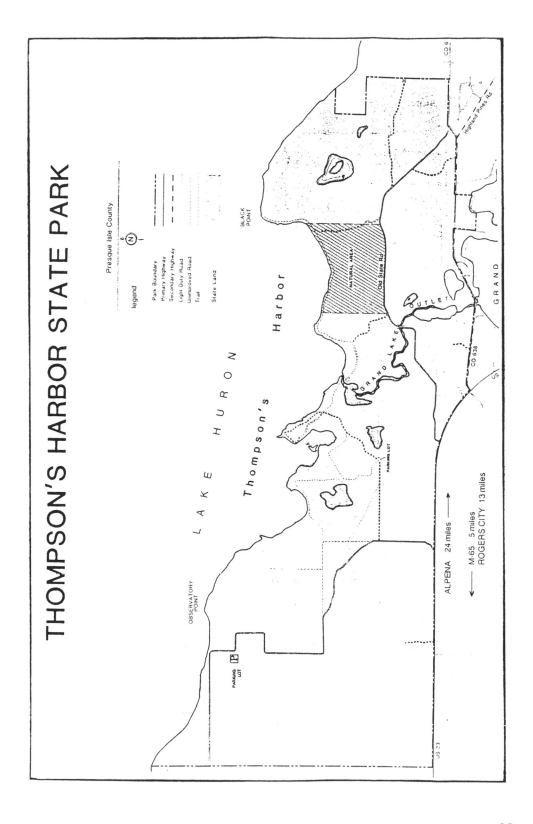

Presque Isle County

N

legend

Park Boundary
Primary Highway
Secondary Highway
Light Duty Road
Unimproved Road
Trail
State Land

BLACK POINT

L A K E   H U R O N

Thompson's   Harbor

GRAND LAKE

NATURAL AREA

Old State Rd

OUTLET

CO 638

US

GRAND

OBSERVATORY POINT

P
PARKING LOT

PARKING LOT

ALPENA 24 miles

M-65 5 miles
ROGERS CITY 13 miles

US 23

CO 6

Highland Pines Rd

WATERLOO RECREATION AREA

Washtenaw and Jackson Counties

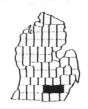

30

A variety of terrain can be enjoyed on the 25 miles of horse trails in the Waterloo Recreation Area. The high trails, which traverse the highest elevation in this part of Michigan, will take you to Pond Lily Overlook and through wooded rolling hills of the southern edge of the park's 20,000 acres. Here you'll see black walnut trees among the pine, oak and maples. The lower trails will take you through an old orchard, fields of goldenrod and other wildflowers, small streams and adjacent to the marshy Baldwin Flood Area. In addition to the regular southern Michigan wildlife, the sandhill crane has residence here.

Horsemen's facilities:
Day use staging area
Toilets
24 rustic campsites
25 miles of marked horse trails
Riding stables nearby on Trist Rd. 313-522-8920

For information:
Waterloo Recreation Area
16345 McClure Rd.
Chelsea, MI 48118
313-475-8307

Fee

Directions: From I-94 exit Clear Lake Rd. (Exit 153). Go north about 1 mile to Harvey Rd. and turn right (east). Go about 1 mile to Loveland Rd. and turn left (north) 2 miles to the entrance to the horseman's camp on the right.

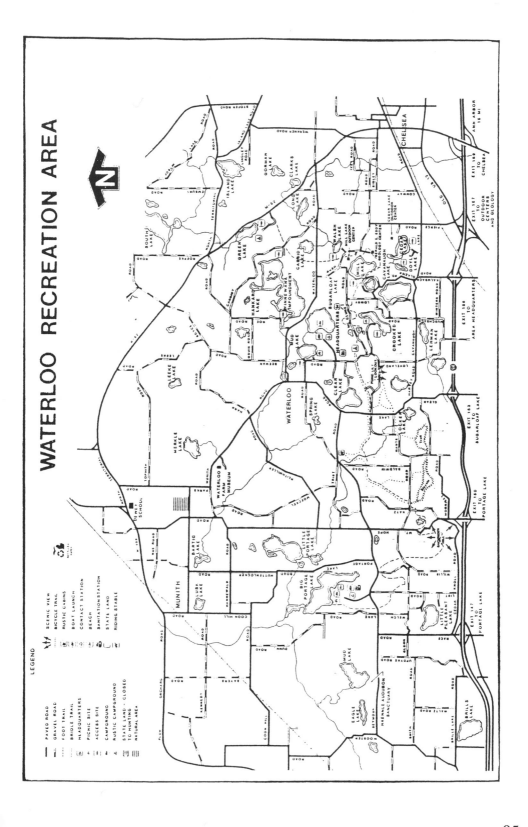

WATERLOO RECREATION AREA

85

31	**WHISKEY CREEK RESORT** **PRIVATE** Mason County - southwest of Scottville	

Whiskey Creek is situated on 1,000 acres of hardwood forest and rolling meadows surrounded by the Manistee National Forest. Two major river systems are within riding distance of the resort.

Horsemen's facilities:
>   Staging area
>   Rustic camping area
>   Water
>   Toilets
>   Restaurants
>   Pool
>   Picket area
>   Marked and unmarked trails through the Manistee National Forest
>   Individual or group camping
>   Maps available

For information & reservations:
>   Whiskey Creek Resort
>   5080 Sippy Rd.
>   Custer, MI 49405
>   616-898-2030

Fee

Directions: From Muskegon, take US 31 north to Pentwater/Monroe exit north of Hart. Head east 7.4 miles on Monroe Rd. to 126th Ave. Turn left 1 mile on 126th and drive north to Madison Rd. Turn right 3.7 miles on Madison to 156th Ave. Turn left on 156th, driving 5 miles to resort (Graver Rd.).

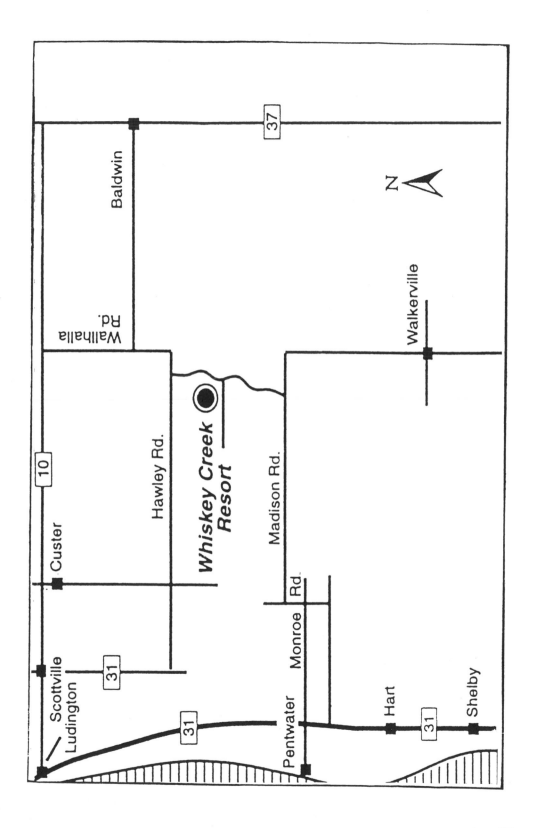

| 32 | **WHITE RIVER TRAIL**
MANISTEE NATIONAL FOREST
Oceana County - Southwest of Hesperia |  |

The White River Trail is located in the White River Foot Travel Area. Its 7,400 acres are an excellent place for recreational activities emphasizing the use of primitive skills. The White River Trail is a multiple-use trail that accommodates year-round use. The trail parallels the beautiful White River and passes through a wide variety of vegetation and also provides opportunities to view a wide range of wildlife.

Note: Please practice no-trace camping

Horsemen's facilities:
Primitive camping area
12 miles of marked trails
Maps available

For information:
District Ranger
White Cloud Ranger District
PO Box 12
White Cloud, MI 49349
616-689-6696
800-721-6263

No fee

Directions: From Hesperia, go west on M-20 about 2 miles to 192nd Ave. Turn left (south) and go 1 mile to Garfield Rd. Turn right (west) and follow signs leading to Pine Point Recreation Area. About .5 mile before the gate to the Pines Point Campground, turn right onto a two-track and park up to 50 ft. off the two-track.

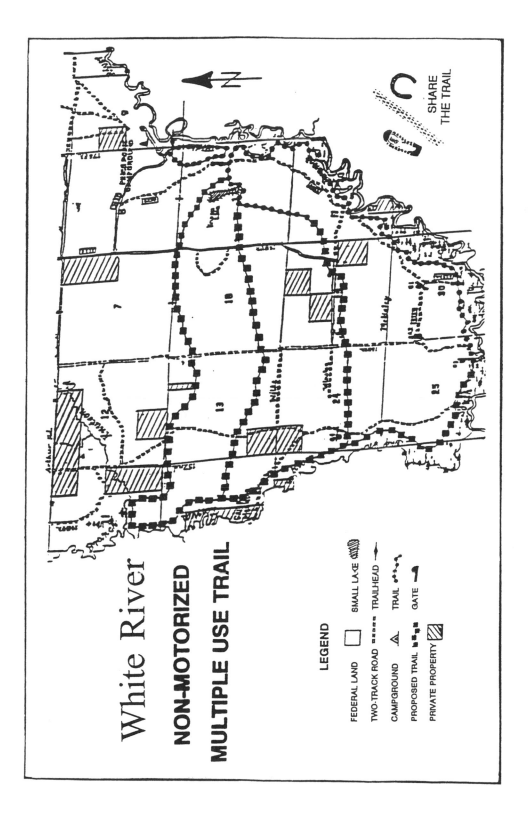

White River
NON-MOTORIZED
MULTIPLE USE TRAIL

SHARE
THE TRAIL

LEGEND

FEDERAL LAND ☐	SMALL LAKE
TWO-TRACK ROAD	TRAILHEAD
CAMPGROUND △	TRAIL
PROPOSED TRAIL	GATE
PRIVATE PROPERTY	

89

33 YANKEE SPRINGS RECREATION AREA & BARRY STATE GAME AREA

Barry County - west of Hastings

The riding trails will take the horseman winding around and to the top of Baird Hill. Then to marshes, Duck Lake, Pines Scenic Area to hilly and wooded terrain through scrub oak, maple, white, red and norfolk pine. Along the way the rider might chance on red, black or gray squirrels, skunks, turkey and a variety of birds or the peace and tranquility the woods or open spaces offer.

Horsemen's facilities:
Day use staging area
25 rustic campsites with tables
Water
Toilets
Picket posts
5 miles of marked trails in Yankee Springs with a connecting link to 9 miles of marked trails in the Barry State Game Area

For information:
Yankee Springs Recreation Area
2104 Gun Lake Rd.
Middleville, MI 49333
616-795-9081

Directions: From US 131 take the Bradley-129th Ave. exit (Exit 61) and go east on 129th Ave. which becomes CR 430. Follow CR 430 (about 11.5 miles total) to CR 611 and turn right (south) about .5 miles to Duffy Rd. Turn right (west) and go less than .5 miles to the horse camp on the left.

90

YANKEE SPRINGS RECREATION AREA

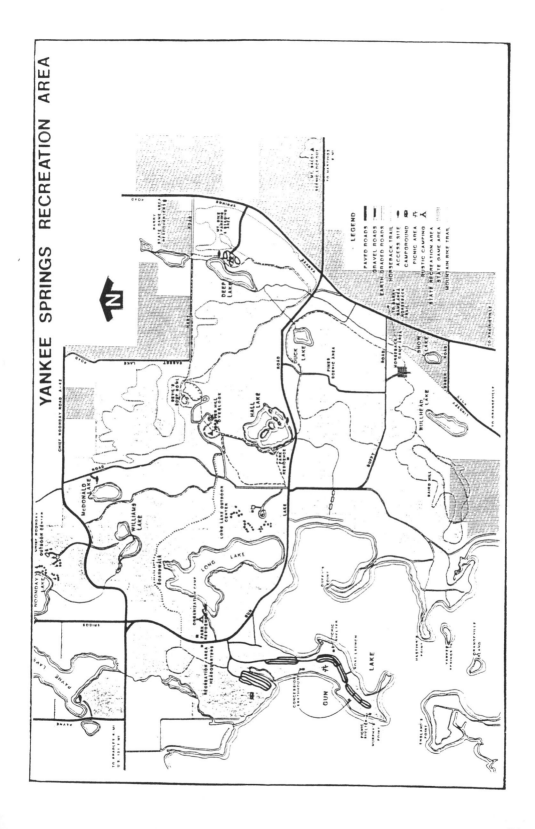

GARY LAKE TRAIL CAMP

34

Benzie County - East of Empire

This is the beginning or ending camp of the Michigan Trail Riders Shore-to-Shore Trail Ride. There are two sections to this camp. There is a lower campground by Gary Lake which is comfortable for a small group of up to 15 rigs. The camp at the top of the hill is flat, open for large groups. The marked trail toward Empire (8.0 miles) is sandy and flat and will take the rider through scrub pine, pine plantations and maple woods on old railroad beds, past an old ski slope and wind its way into Empire. The marked trail to the south will be sandy, winding over rolling hills through maple and pine woods. One can ride to Lake DuBonnet Camp about 18 miles on this trail (marked with blue dots).

Horsemen's facilities:
Rustic campsites
Picket posts
Water
Toilets

For information:
Department of Natural Resources
15200 Honor Highway
Beulah, MI 49617
616-325-4611

No fee

Directions: From Empire, about 5 miles on M-72 turn right (south) on Plowman Road. Go about 2 miles and turn left (east) on Pettingill Road and continue to the camp on the right side of the road. Watch for sign to trail camp. From east - Traverse City on M-72 - travel about 13 miles from where M-22 goes north from M-72 to 669 (Maple City Road) and turn left (south). Go 1.0 miles to Pettingill Road and turn right (west) and go about 2.25 miles to trail camp on left. The lower camping area is by the lake, the upper camp is used for trail rides.

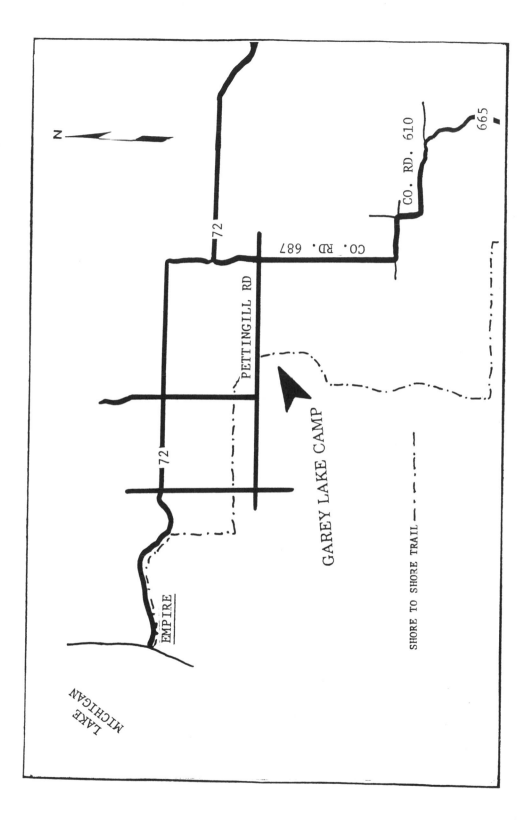

N

LAKE
MICHIGAN

EMPIRE

72

72

PETTINGILL RD

CO. RD. 687

CO. RD. 610

665

GAREY LAKE CAMP

SHORE TO SHORE TRAIL — · — · —

93

	LAKE DUBONNET
35	**(MUD LAKE) CAMP**
	Grand Traverse County - near Interlochen

Lake DuBonnet Camp is one of the Shore-to-Shore Trail camps. This is a comfortable camp as it is shaded and offers many scenic sites close to the lake. There are unmarked trails and marked trails over flat sandy terrain through pine, maple, birch and beech woods. The Shore-to-Shore Trail leads either to Gary Lake camp west) or to Scheck's Camp (east).

Horsemen's facilities:
> Rustic campsites
> Picket posts
> Water
> Toilets
> Marked and unmarked trails

For information:
> Department of Natural Resources
> 15200 Honor Highway
> Beulah, MI 49617
> 616-325-4611

Fee

Directions: From US 31 and M-37 junction south of Traverse City, go west 7 miles on US 31 to Wildwood Rd. turn right (north) and go 1 mile. Turn left (west) and go .5 miles. Turn right (north) and go .25 miles across the dam. Turn right (east) along the water into camp.

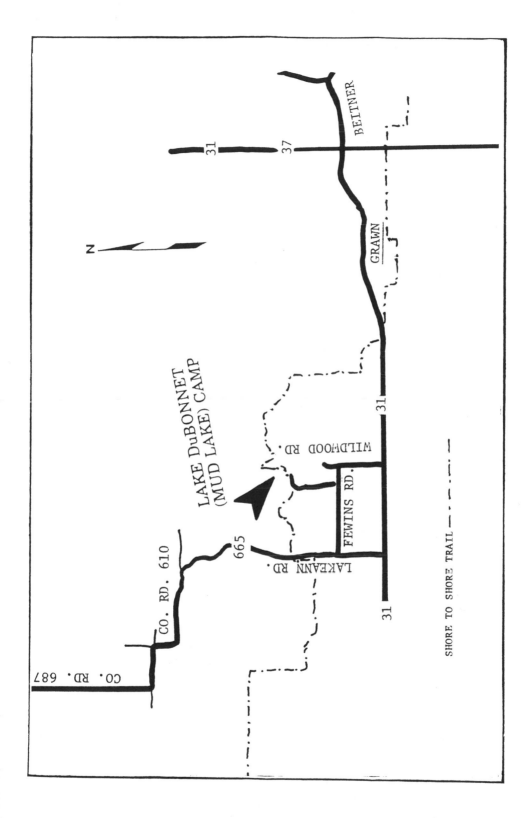

N

31
37

BETTNER

GRAWN

31

WILDWOOD RD.

LAKE DuBONNET
(MUD LAKE) CAMP

FEWINS RD.

LAKEANN RD.

665

CO. RD. 610

CO. RD. 687

31

SHORE TO SHORE TRAIL — · — · —

36 SCHECK'S TRAIL CAMP

Grand Traverse County
Southeast of Traverse City

Scheck's Trail Camp is part of the Shore-to-Shore Trail network. This camp is one of 4 or 5 of the trail camps that receive extended use. Many horsepeople choose to use Sheck's as a place to stay and enjoy the numerous marked and unmarked trails in the area. You may chose to ride west to Mayfield on a flat, sandy relatively straight trail for ice cream; or northwest on one of three rolling sandy single track, a two-track or a snowmobile trail to explore the riding area along the Boardman River, or for a visit to Ranch Rudolf.

Horsemen's facilities
Rustic campsites
Toilets
Picket posts
Water
Marked and unmarked trails
Snowmobile trails

For information:
Department of Natural Resources
404 W. 14th St.
Traverse City, MI 49684
616-922-5280

Fee

Directions: From US 131 and S. Boardman junction travel west on Boardman Rd.. and Supply Rd.. about 6 miles to Brown Bridge Rd.. Turn left (south) and go about 3.5 miles to the camp on the left. Watch for trail camp sign. From the west - via Highway 37 and Highway 31 (Chum's Corner) go east on Beitner Rd.. about 1.6 miles to River Rd.. and turn right. Follow River Rd.. about 6.5 miles and it will become Brown Bridge Rd.. Go straight and the trail camp will be about 4 miles on the right side of the road. Watch for trail camp sign.

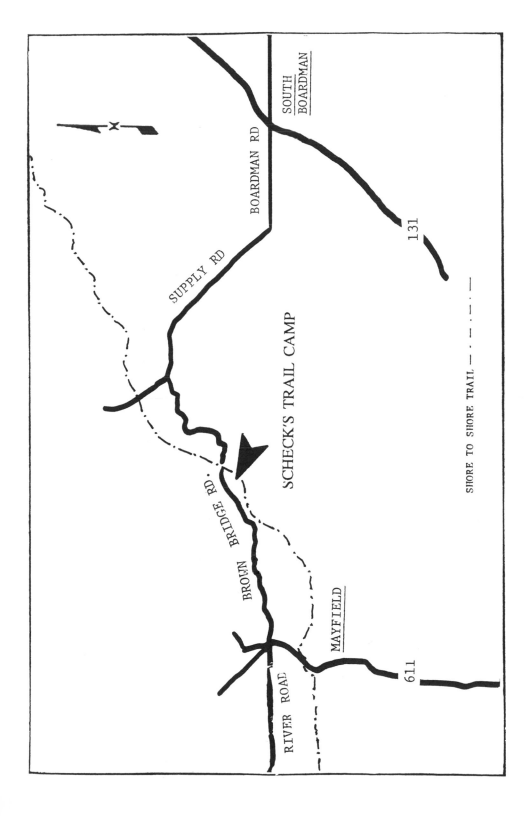

SHORE TO SHORE TRAIL — · — · —

SCHECK'S TRAIL CAMP

SOUTH BOARDMAN

BOARDMAN RD

SUPPLY RD

BROWN BRIDGE RD.

MAYFIELD

RIVER ROAD

131

611

KALKASKA TRAIL CAMP

37 Kalkaska County - just north of Kalkaska

Kalkaska Camp is another camp on the Shore-to-Shore Trail. This is a trail camp. A place for horses and people to rest. On the west trail out of camp is the Little Rapid River where you can take a short ride to water your horse. If you're riding the Short-to-Shore Trail to Scheck's Camp, this is one of the most scenic areas of the entire trail. The east trail out of camp goes through pine plantations. If you're riding toward Goose Creek Camp you will pass through the Mayhem Swamp and the sands of Kalkaska County.

Horsemen's facilities:
Rustic campsites
Water
Toilets
Picket posts
East/West marked Shore-to-Shore trail

For information:
Department of Natural Resources
2089 N. Birch
Kalkaska, MI 49646
616-258-2711

Fee

Directions: From the junction of US 131 and CR 612 in Kalkaska go north on US 131 about .25 miles. Turn left (northwest) on the Beebe Rd. and go about .75 miles to Metzger Rd. Turn left (west) and go about 1 mile. Turn left (south) on Rice Rd. and go .25 miles to camp entrance.

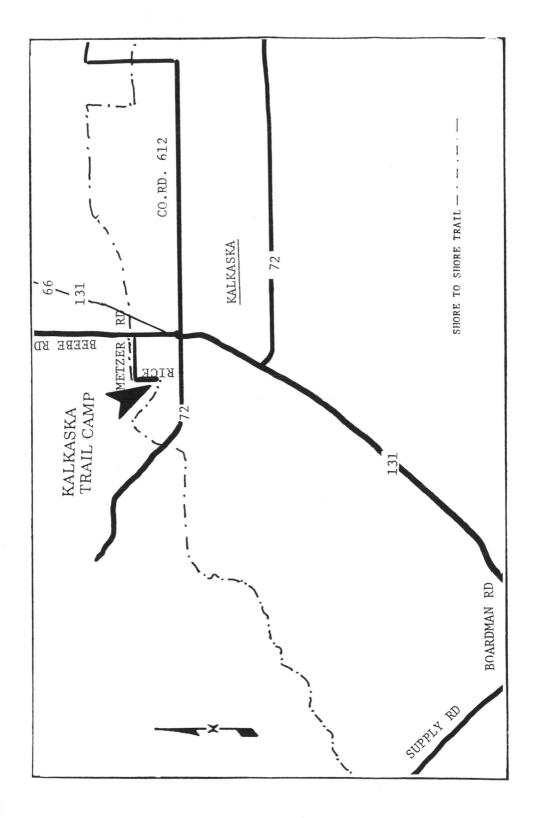

	GOOSE CREEK TRAIL CAMP	
38	Crawford County - Northwest of Grayling	

If you ask trail riders to pick their favorite horse camp, Goose Creek would be at the top of the list or close to it. It's an all-purpose trail camp. There is lots of room for parking and plenty of space to picket horses. You can take a ride to Fredrick for lunch; or to M-72 for ice cream. There are trails north, south, east or west. You can take large circle rides or small circle rides. Ride the flats or the rolling hills to see water, wildlife, and woods. Trail riders can stay for days and ride a different trail each day. In the summer bring a tube to float down the Manistee River.

Note: No horses are allowed on banks or in river except at crossing.

Horsemen's facilities:
Rustic campsites
    Water
    Toilets
    Picket posts
    Marked (East/West Short-to-Shore) and unmarked two-tracks and snowmobile trails

For information:
    Department of Natural Resources
    1955 N. I-75 Business Loop
    Grayling, MI 48738
    517-348-6371

Fee

Directions: From Grayling go west on M-72 about 7 miles to Manistee River Road and turn right (north). Go about 6 miles to Goose Creek Camp on the left. Or, from County Road 612 and Manistee River Road go south on Manistee River Road about .3 of a mile and turn right into the camp.

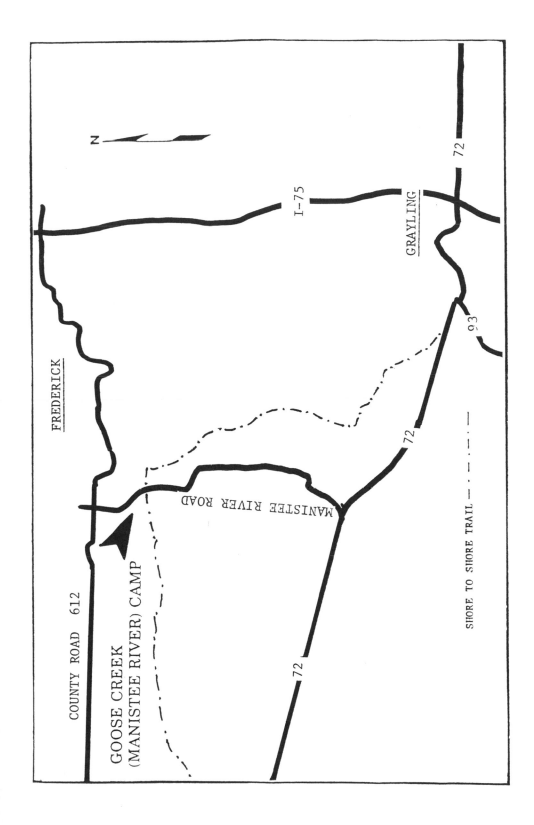

N

FREDERICK

GRAYLING

I-75

72

93

72

72

COUNTY ROAD 612

GOOSE CREEK
(MANISTEE RIVER) CAMP

MANISTEE RIVER ROAD

SHORE TO SHORE TRAIL — · — · —

FOUR MILE TRAIL CAMP

39

Crawford County - Southeast of Grayling

This is a trail camp. You and your horse can take time to rest. From here, the Shore-to-Shore Trail goes east and west. For circle riding, other camps are more appealing with a greater variety of trail choices. To the west is flat riding, toward Camp Grayling, on sand trails with stands of oak and pines mixed with clear cuts. To the east, Huron National Forest, with single tracks and two-tracks going to the South Branch of the Au Sable River. If you're traveling with your horse on I-75 and need a convenient place to spend the night, this is it.

Horsemen's facilities:
Rustic campsites
Water
Toilets
Picket posts
Shore-to-Shore Trail

For information:
Department of Natural Resources
1955B I-75 Business Loop
Grayling, MI

No fee

Directions: From I-75 and Four Mile interchange, go east on Four Mile Road about four miles. Turn right (south) into the camp. From Luzerne coming west on 72, go about 16 miles from Ma Deeter's to Stephan Bridge Rd. Turn left (south) and go about four miles to Four Mile Rd. and turn right. The camp is about 2.75 miles on the left.

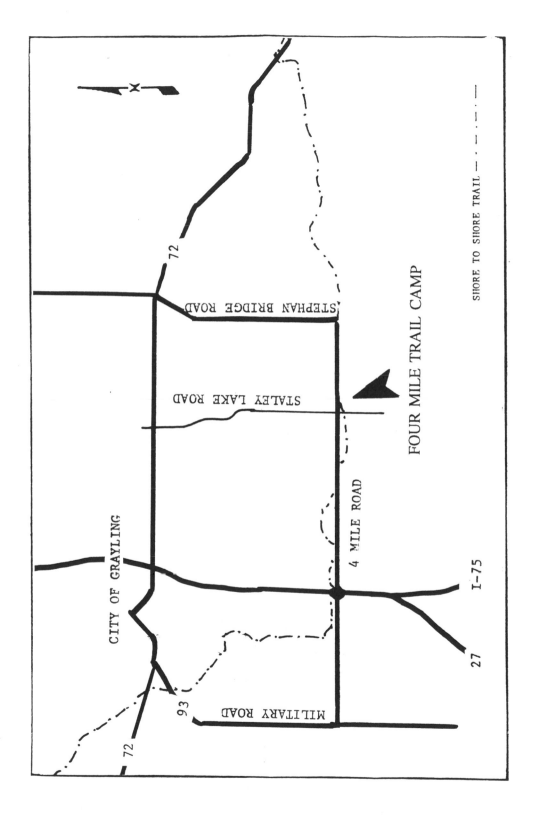

SHORE TO SHORE TRAIL — · — · —

FOUR MILE TRAIL CAMP

STEPHAN BRIDGE ROAD

STALEY LAKE ROAD

4 MILE ROAD

CITY OF GRAYLING

MILITARY ROAD

72

93

72

27

I-75

LUZERNE TRAIL CAMP

40

Oscoda County - near Luzerne

This is a pleasant horsemen's camp. It's one of the Shore-to-Shore Trail camps but it offers the horseman choices of trails and activities. You may enjoy the short ride to Luzerne for desires of the palate or ride east to the Luzerne Bridge through and over the swamp, a very picturesque area. If you follow the marked trail to the west you will ride a winding rolling single track through clear cuts, new growth and maturing woods. This is also the trail segment that connects to the North-South Riding/Hiking Trail.

Note: At the Luzerne Trail Bridge, there is one way horse traffic on the day the camp-to-camp riders are using the bridge during the Shore-to-Shore rides.

Horsemen's facilities:
    Rustic campsites
    Water
    Toilets
    Picket posts
    Marked and unmarked trails
    Group camp available by reservation

For information:
    US Forest Service District Ranger
    Huron National Forest
    Mio, MI 48647
    517-826-3717

Directions: From the intersection of M-72 and Deeter Road (blinker light) go south on Deeter Road 1.5 miles (road will turn west about .75 miles from town) to Durfee Road. Turn left (watch for trail camp sign) and go .75 miles to camp entrance. Turn left into camp.

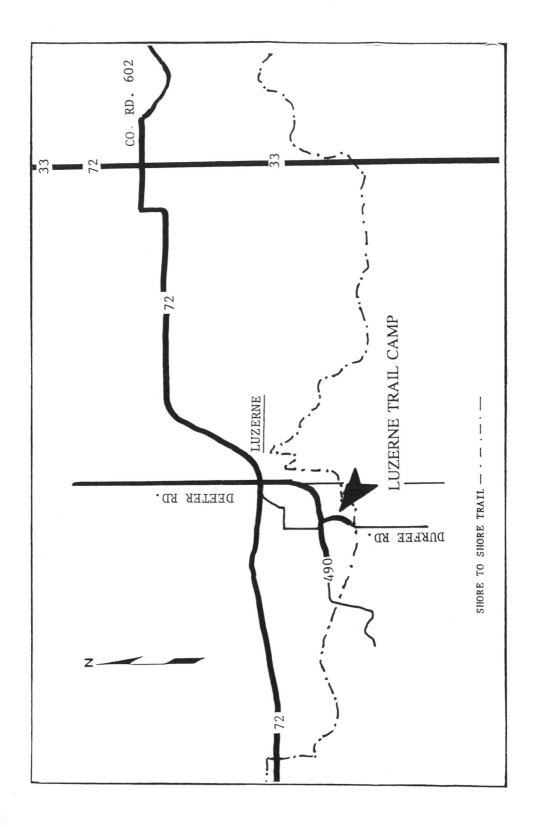

105

MC KINLEY TRAIL CAMP

41

Oscoda County - east of Mio

McKinley Camp is a trail camp on the Shore-to-Shore Trail. There are trails other than the Shore-to-Shore Trail. A ride to the river is pleasant. The Shore-to-Shore Trail to the west is rolling and scenic taking the rider through a variety of terrain, tree growth and woods. The ride to the east and southeast to South Branch Camp is one of the most picturesque of the Shore-to-Shore Trails with the possibility of seeing the American Bald Eagle along the Au Sable River and Alcona Dam Pond, and the work of the proverbial "busy beaver."

Horsemen's facilities:
   Rustic campsites
   Water
   Toilets
   Picket posts
   Marked and unmarked trails

For information:
   US Forest Service District Ranger
   Mio, MI 48647
   517-826-3717

No fee

Directions: From the Mio intersection of M-72 and M-33 and CR 602 (blinking light), go east on CR 602 about 9 miles and turn left into camp drive (watch for trail camp sign and turn). Camp is about 1 mile back. From McKinley go south across the river on Evans Road to CR 602 and go to the right about 1.5 miles to the trail camp sign. Turn right and the camp is about 1 mile from the road.

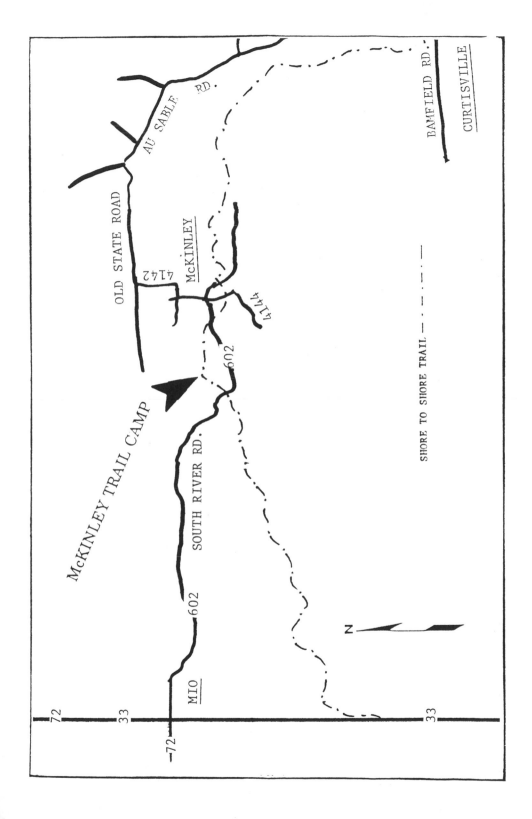

MCKINLEY TRAIL CAMP

OLD STATE ROAD

AU SABLE RD.

McKINLEY

4142

4144

602

SOUTH RIVER RD.

602

MIO

72

33

33

72

72

33

BAMFIELD RD.

CURTISVILLE

SHORE TO SHORE TRAIL — · — · —

N

42 SOUTH BRANCH CAMP
Iosco County - east of South Branch

South Branch Trail Camp is a comfortable camp located along the South Branch River. It gets a little crowded when a full trail ride is using the camp. You can ride in a northern direction to a scenic overlook of Alcona Dam Pond or ride along the South Branch River. This is one of the trail camps where there is a variety or riding and comfortable campsites.

Horsemen's facilities:
Rustic campsites
Water
Toilets
Picket posts
Marked and unmarked trails
Group camp by reservation only

For information:
US Forest Service District Ranger
Huron National Forest
Mio, MI 49647
517-826-3717

Fee

Directions: From the intersection of M-65 and Rollaway Rd.., go north about 2 miles. Turn right into the campground.

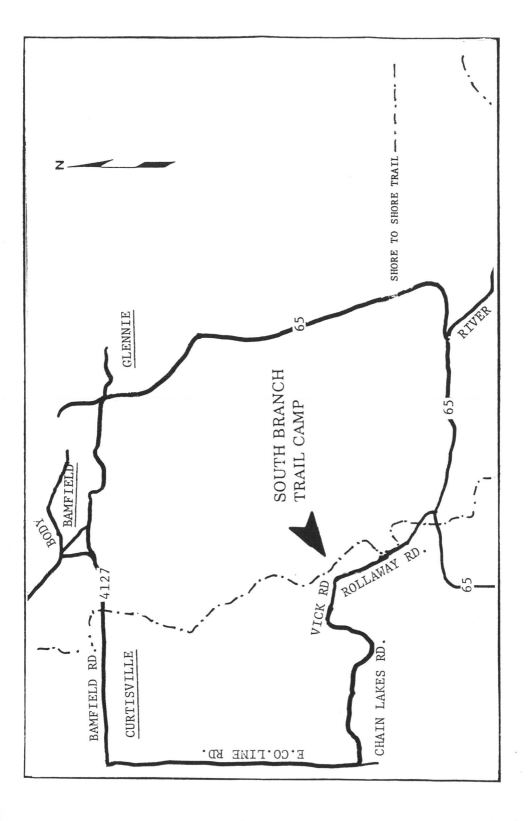

N

GLENNIE

BAMFIELD

BODY

SHORE TO SHORE TRAIL

65

SOUTH BRANCH
TRAIL CAMP

RIVER

65

65

VICK RD.

ROLLAWAY RD.

CHAIN LAKES RD.

4127

BAMFIELD RD.

CURTISVILLE

E.CO.LINE RD.

OLD ORCHARD COUNTY PARK
Iosco County - near Oscoda

This is a county park located between the Foote Dam Pond and River Rd.., in the Huron National Forest. The rider can experience flat land riding through scrub oak, pine and hardwoods and view Lake Huron to the east. To the west is a 2 mile ridge trail overlooking the pond before it continues into the Huron National Forest. This camp is used at times for the Shore-to-Shore ride.

Horsemen's facilities:
Camping sites
Picket posts
Toilets
Showers
Picnic tables with fire rings
Beach
Pavilion
Marked and unmarked trails
Full-time recreation department during the summer

For information:
Old Orchard Park
PO Box 368
Oscoda, MI 48750
517-739-7814

Fee

Directions: 881 E. River Rd.., 8.5 miles west of Oscoda or 13 miles east of M-65.

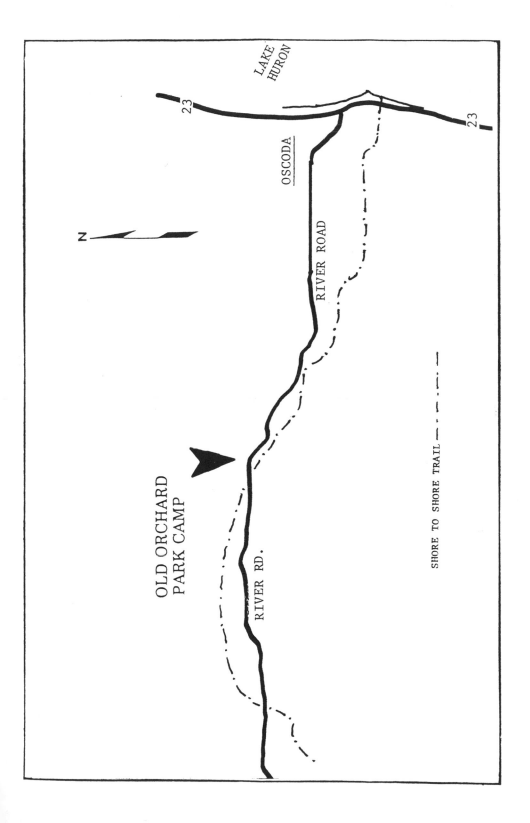

111

WALSH ROAD TRAIL CAMP

44 Crawford County - northeast of Grayling

This is a new trail camp of the north spur of the Michigan Riding/Hiking Trail. The trail rider will be riding through a variety of terrains to and from this camp including plains, hardwoods, marshes and along the Big Creek River. At this time, there is very little circle riding.

Horsemen's facilities:
9 rustic campsites
Water
Toilet
Picket posts
Group camping area with permit

For information:
Grayling Area Forest Manager
1955 N. I-75 BL
Grayling, MI 49738
517-348-6371

Directions: From M-72 in Luzerne (east from Grayling, west from M-10) take CR 489 north to CR 608. Turn left (west) 4 miles to Walsh Rd. Turn right (north) and go 4.5 miles to the camp.

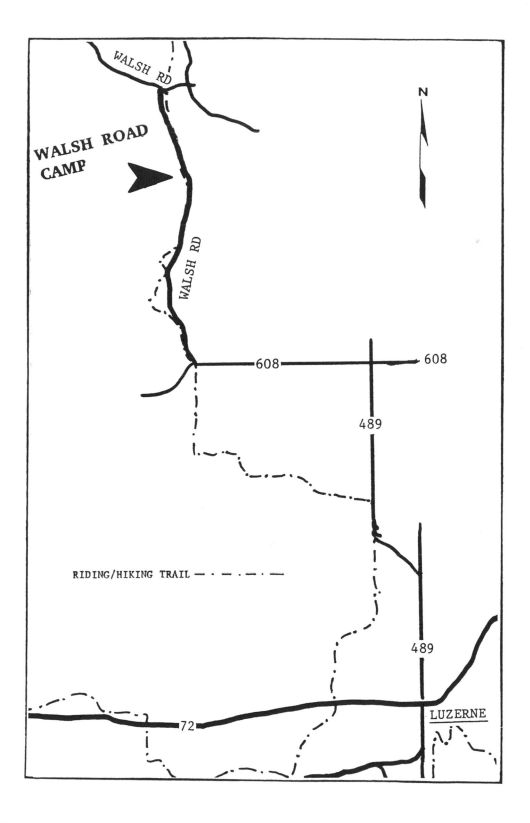

45 | JOHNSON'S CROSSING TRAIL CAMP
Otsego County - west of Gaylord

This trail camp opened in 1995 to help alleviate the overuse of Elk Hill Campground. This site was selected not only because of the close proximity to Elk Hill but also because of the enchantment of the Pigeon River Country area with its swamps, aspen stands, and stands of red and white pine. In essence, every forest type in the state of Michigan can be found here. A day circle ride will take you into the south Pigeon River Country Area.

Horsemen's facilities:
    7 campsites
    Well
    Toilet
    Picket posts
    Group camp area available by reservation (call area office)

For information:
    Pigeon River Country Forest Area
    1966 Twin Lakes Rd.
    Vanderbilt, MI 49795

Fee

Directions: From Gaylord, take M-32 east to Gingell Rd. (about 12 miles from I-75). Turn left (north) and go about 4 miles to Sparr Rd. Turn right (east) and go about 2 miles to Johnson's Crossing Rd. Turn right (east) and go about 2 miles to the camp.

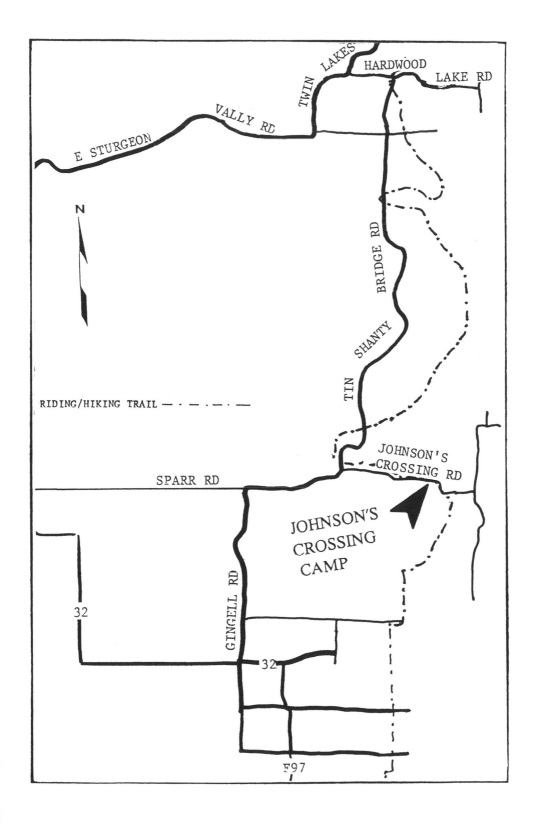

ELK HILL TRAIL CAMP

46 Otsego County - east of Vanderbilt

The Elk Hill Camp offers the horseman an opportunity to ride in an area that is as pristine and picturesque as anywhere in Michigan. The panoramic views offer rolling hills and prairies, cedar swamps, pine plantations, clear cuts, creeks and rivers. There is also an abundance of animal life - from the usual rabbits, squirrels and deer to the unusual elk. The elk population is a bit shy, but you can often view any number at about dusk on horseback of you're in the right location. In the spring you can search for morel mushrooms and a great variety of wildflowers from horseback.

Note: If Elk Hill Camp is full (10 sites available) Johnson's Crossing Campground (7 sites) is about a forty minute drive south; or, Stoney Creek Campground (10 sites) is about a 60 minute drive north. Both offer excellent riding opportunities. Another choice is to follow instructions for camping in an undesignated camping area and camp in a state forest. See Appendix.

Horsemen's facilities:
   10 rustic campsites
   Water
   Toilets
   Picket posts
   Group site available by reservation only (call or write forest area office)
   Marked North-South Riding/Hiking Trail

For information:
   Pigeon River Country State Forest
   9966 Twin Lakes Rd.
   Vanderbilt, MI 49795
   517-983-4101

Fee

Directions: From I-75 in Vanderbilt go east on Main St. to blinker light and turn left (east). This is Sturgeon Valley Rd. Go about 11.2 miles to Twin Lakes Rd. (Round Lake Campground Rd.) and turn left (north), go about 2 miles and turn left into campground.

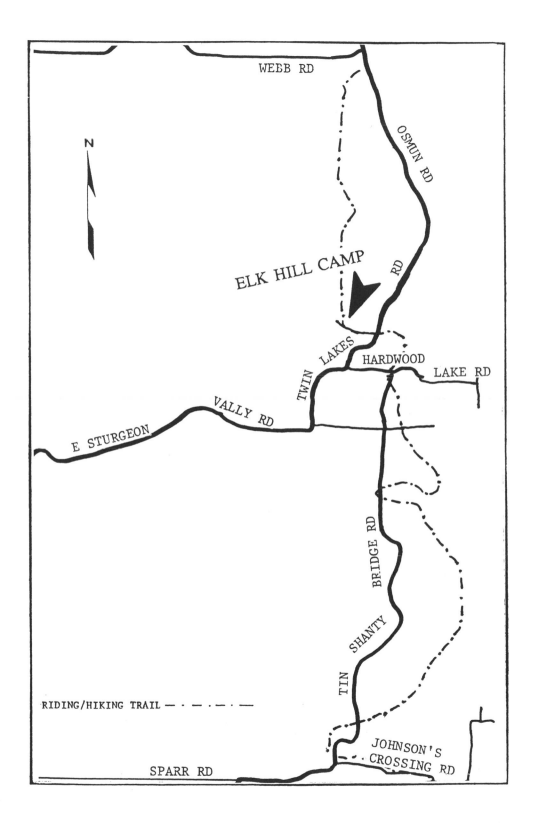

WEBB RD

N

OSMUN RD

ELK HILL CAMP

RD

TWIN LAKES

HARDWOOD

LAKE RD

VALLY RD

E STURGEON

BRIDGE RD

TIN SHANTY

RIDING/HIKING TRAIL — · — · —

JOHNSON'S
CROSSING RD

SPARR RD

117

STONEY CREEK CAMP
Cheboygan County - east of Indian River

In 1995, this camp was added to the North-South Hiking/Riding Trail. The trail passes over rolling terrain through hardwoods and pine and over a bridge that splits the floodwaters from the river. There are lots of two-tracks, flatlands and riding along the river in this new camp area. Marked trails for day circle rides are intended for the Stoney Creek Camp.

Horsemen's facilities:
   9 rustic campsites
   Toilets
   Picket posts
   Group camp by reservation only

For information:
   Indian River Forest Area
   PO Box 10
   Indian River, MI 49749
   616-238-9313

Fee

Directions: From Indian River (I-75) take M-68 east about 8 miles to the junction of M-68 and M-33. Turn left (north) 2 miles on M-33 and continue 200 feet past Quincy Street (mobile home community). Turn right and go .75 miles to camp.

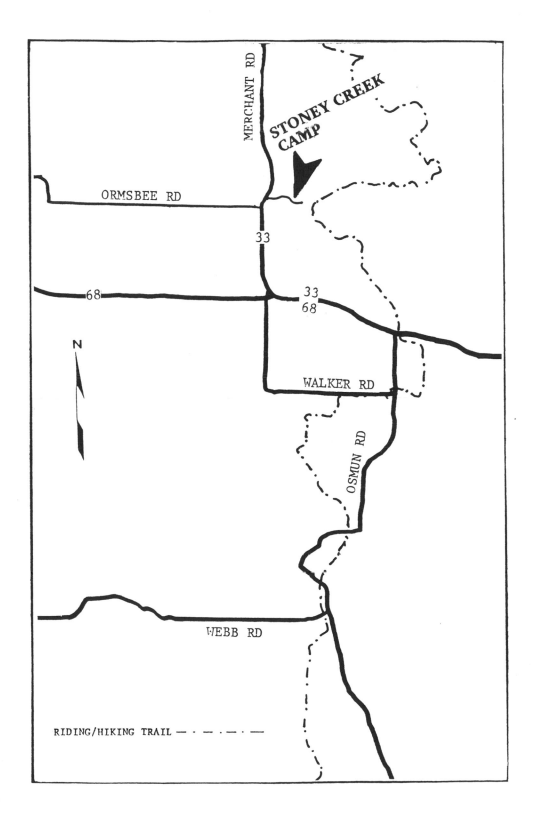

48 HOPKINS CREEK TRAIL CAMP
Missaukee County - northeast of Manton

Hopkins Creek Trail Camp is located along the bank of Hopkins Creek. This camp is flat and spread among the hardwood, pine and brush. This camp draws horse families and groups from the central and western side of the state to enjoy a pleasant camping area. The camp is located on the north/south spur of the Michigan Riding Hiking Trail. The trail north to Scheck's camp begins at the Hopkins Creek camp.

Horsemen's facilities:
Rustic campsites
Water
Toilets
Picket posts
Marked trail to Scheck's camp and unmarked single and two-track trails

For information:
Department of Natural Resources
2089 N. Birch
Kalkaska, MI 49646
616-258-2711

Fee

Directions: From US 131 and M-42 in Manton go east about 6 miles to Lucas Road. Turn left (north) and go about 6 miles. Just after you pass over Hopkins Creek take the road on the left about 1.5 miles to the camp area.

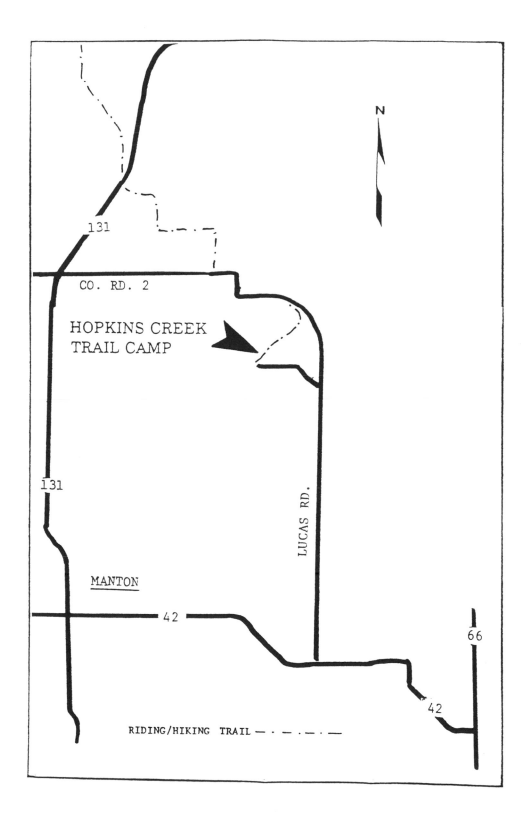

N

131

CO. RD. 2

HOPKINS CREEK
TRAIL CAMP

LUCAS RD.

131

MANTON

42

66

42

RIDING/HIKING TRAIL — · — · — · —

APPENDICES

TRAIL RIDERS CHECKLIST

The following is a list of items you may want to bring on a trail ride. The items you pack may vary, depending on your situation - whether you're planning on camping under the stars or sleeping in a motorhome or camper. It's a good idea to check off the items as you load them.

VEHICLE

_____air pump
_____auxiliary gas tank or can & funnel
_____brake fluid
_____directions to camp
_____electrical wire & tape
_____fan belt
_____fire extinguisher (a MUST!)
_____first aid kit
_____flashlight & batteries
_____jack (bumper or axle)
_____jumper cables
_____lug wrench
_____maps (road &/or forestry)
_____pliers
_____shovel
_____spare tire (another MUST!)
_____tire pressure gauge
_____tongue hoist wheel
_____tools
_____tow chain
_____water (for man, horse & radiator)

HORSE

_____blanket
_____breast collar
_____bridle or hackamore
_____cinch
_____curry comb
_____first aid supplies
_____halter
_____hobbles
_____hoof picks
_____insect repellent
_____leadropes
_____leather punch
_____leather straps/strings (repair tack)
_____pellet tote bag/feed bag/bucket
_____picket line/high line
_____saddle bags
_____saddle
_____saddle pads
_____salt
_____spurs
_____twitch
_____water bucket

CAMPING GEAR

_____bedroll
_____binoculars
_____canteen
_____cleaning rags
_____clothes pins
_____fishing poles & lures
_____ground cloth/waterproof tarp
_____lawn chair
_____notebook & pencil
_____pocket knife
_____rubbish bags
_____scissors
_____sewing kit
_____shelter
_____tie rope for bedroom & duffle

PERSONAL GEAR

_____antibiotic ointment
_____bandanna or handkerchief
_____bathing suit
_____boots
_____camera & film & batteries
_____comb/hair brush
_____deodorant
_____duffle bag
_____galoshes
_____glasses (optical/sun)
_____gloves
_____hand soap & case
_____hat (& tiedown for windy weather)
_____insect repellent
_____jacket
_____lip balm
_____medications
_____pants
_____sandwich baggies
_____shaving equipment
_____shirts (for all weather conditions)
_____shoes (for around camp)
_____shorts
_____slicker or poncho
_____small mirror
_____socks
_____suntan lotion
_____tissue (toilet)
_____toothbrush & paste
_____towels (bath)
_____watch/alarm clock

TRAIL ETHICS

With increasing demands for recreational trails, many trails may be multi-use. Mutual concern for safety and trail maintenance will help maintain goodwill and cooperation among all trail users. We suggest that equestrian trail users follow these ethics.

1. If the ride has a trail boss, they have authority on the trail. Riders should stay behind the trail boss or ride on their own.
2. Stallions should be marked with a yellow ribbon prominently displayed on their tail. (Stallions may be restricted on commercial and other organized rides; please check with the trail boss.)
3. All pets, including dogs and cats, should be kept on leashes.
4. No horse should be allowed to chew trees or other vegetation. Take any necessary precaution to prevent this.
5. If your horse kicks, you must tie a red ribbon on the horse's tail.
6. Horses must remain under control. No running (full out gallop) should be permitted around other horses, pedestrians and trail users.
7. Improperly trained and aggressive horses should be excused from all groups and trails.
8. No trash will be left on the trails...this includes cigarette butts, etc. Pack it out with you!
9. Tack must be properly maintained. Makeshift type repairs are reserved for temporary use only.
10. Riding double is not safe and is discouraged.
11. Rough riding or racing should be done away from the group. If you need to pass, do so slowly after the group has been asked and has gotten off the trail.
12. All horses must have a negative Coggins test within one year of the ride.
13. When on the trail, try to keep a horse-length between you and the horse in front of you.
14. Courtesy is imperative. Do not remove or rearrange any trail markers. Stay on the designated trail.

MANURE: Remove all manure from the parking area; carry a shovel, broom and garbage bags in your trailer.

RIGHT OF WAY: Horses, cyclist and hikers with backpacks may be frightening and unfamiliar to each other. Cooperation, education and courtesy are necessary.

1. When meeting each other on trails, all trail users will move to the right of the trail.
2. Hikers and cyclists should yield the right-of-way to horses. Cyclists may need to dismount for safe passage.
3. The faster moving trail user will have the right-of-way to pass in a safe method.
4. Trail users seeking to pass will indicate verbally their desire and wait until safe passage is possible. Horses may need to be dismounted or moved off the trail.

A NOTE ON HORSE SHOPPING
Reprinted with permission from *The Right Lead* by Kaye April

More and more people are becoming "first-time" horse owners, either because they want to learn to ride, or their children have joined 4H or a spouse is joining in this pleasureful sport. I think this is wonderful, however, I would like to caution people buying a horse for the first time; please learn all you can <u>first</u> by asking lots of questions of horse owning friends or neighbors or by going to stables who offer lessons and/or training and asking LOTS OF QUESTIONS!

You also should decide what you will be doing with the horse; is it going to be used for pleasure riding, showing (halter or performance), jumping, dressage or breeding? The only thing horses have in common is that they all have four legs, a mane and tail! Each breed has been developed for specific purpose, although some breeds can be used for multiple purposes. The next questions is: "Do I want a registered or unregistered horse?" If you will be pleasure riding or showing at 4H or open shows, you may decide on a "grade" horse. This is a horse that is unregistered either because it's parentage is not known or, perhaps, the horse is of "mixed" parentage that would make it unregisterable. This does not by any means make the horse "undesirable." There are many people who would not sell their grade horse for any price! For a first horse, I almost always suggest that you find an older, well-broke horse. It is not fun having a horse that is as green as you are and, in fact, can turn you off horses for the rest of your life!

Always take a friend or knowledgeable person with you when looking at a horse. If the horse has a regular stall, look at the stall to see if there are signs of the wood having been chewed or kicked. Ask if the horse has any barn vices that you need to know about. When the horse is being groomed and saddled, does it stand calmly and quietly? Does it need to be worked on the longe line before riding or can you mount and quietly walk off with it? Have the owner ride the horse and show it at all gaits in both directions. No matter how calm and sweet the horse is, the most important thing is, "Do YOU feel comfortable on this horse?" If you aren't at ease on the horse, DON'T BUY IT! It may be that you need some lessons to help you gain confidence but it may be more of your "gut instinct" telling you that this is not the horse for you. Horses can sense when a person is uncomfortable and this can make some horses uncomfortable, too. If you feel uncomfortable riding with a friend or trainer along with you, how will you handle the horse once you get it home and are on your own? I have almost always operated on the old premise of, "When in doubt, DON'T." Don't be afraid to say no, don't let anyone make up your mind for you, and don't buy anything if you have any doubts! A new horse and rider are not a team immediately; however, to become a team, you must feel some rapport with each other. Don't give up on finding the "right horse," it's waiting for you in someone's barn! Good luck!

FEES

On U.S. Forest Service property:

1. There is no charge for camping on federal land, except where posted.
2. Use only down or dead trees for firewood.
3. Use soap away from rivers and lakes.
4. No trace camping.

In Michigan State Parks:

    Day Pass: $4
    Season Pass: $20
    Michigan Resident 65 or over: $5
    Horse campground: $10

In a Michigan State Forest <u>designated</u> area (horse camping):

    $6 - pay post

To camp free in an <u>undesignated</u> (other than a designated campground) area of a Michigan State Forest :

1. Get an Act 48 card (camping permit) from a Department of Natural Resources office (listed herein).
2. Locate and park/camp on state land.
3. Park outside the road right-of-way.
4. Read instructions and post your permit.
5. Do not cut live trees.
6. Obey all rules and regulations.
7. When you leave, leave permit posted.
8. Practice no trace camping - when you have gone, no one knows you were there.
9. Have fun!

Note: A state forest camp site is defined as an area for one wheeled camping unit and one tent or six people maximum per site.

CAMP REGISTRATION CARD

REQUIRED UNDER AUTHORITY OF ACT 48, P. A. 1952, AS AMENDED.

INSTRUCTIONS:

1. *Print* all requested information in *pencil* in plain and legible English. Include the name and complete address of each member of the camping party.
2. Prominently post this card at the camp site **before** making camp and leave posted upon departure when camping on State-owned land other than State Parks, Recreation Areas, State Forest Camprounds or State Game Area Campgrounds. Do not post on a motor home, camper or trailer; post elsewhere on camping site.
3. Every member of the party shall be responsible for disposal of all rubbish and litter of any nature brought into or built upon the premises by the camping party.

VIOLATION OF THE ABOVE REGULATIONS IS PUNISHABLE BY A FINE OF UP TO $100.00 AND COSTS AND/OR 90 DAYS IN JAIL.

INFORMATION: Camp means the erection of a tent or tent-type camper or the parking and occupancy of a travel or house trailer or truck camper. It is unlawful to camp in one location more than 15 days from May 1 to Labor Day or more than 20 days from Labor day to May 1 without permission. It is also unlawful to camp on State-owned lands within one mile of a State Forest Campground.

NAME	STREET ADDRESS , CITY, STATE & ZIP CODE

ARRIVAL DATE: DEPARTURE DATE::

TYPE OF CAMP: ☐ TENT ☐ HOUSE TRAILER ☐ TENT CAMPER ☐ PICKUP CAMPER ☐ OTHER

VEHICLE LICENSE NUMBER:	STATE	TRAILER LICENSE NUMBER:	STATE

COMPLETE THE FOLLOWING THE SAME AS ABOVE

NAME	STREET ADDRESS , CITY, STATE & ZIP CODE

ARRIVAL DATE: DEPARTURE DATE:

VEHICLE LICENSE NUMBER:	STATE	TRAILER LICENSE NUMBER:	STATE

LEAVE BLANK - FOR OFFICER USE ONLY

LOCATION OF CAMP:

PR 1313 (Rev. 4/95)

DO NOT DETACH THIS PORTION OF CARD

132

MICHIGAN DEPARTMENT OF NATURAL RESOURCES

FOREST MANAGEMENT DIVISION
Office of the State Forester, Mason Building, 8th Floor, PO Box 30452, Lansing, MI 48909-7952
517-373-1275

Forest Fire Experiment Station, PO Box 68, Roscommon, MI 48653; 517-275-5211

Copper County State Forest (District 1): US 41 North, Box 440, Baraga, MI 49908; 906-353-6651
   Baraga Forest Area: US 41 N., Box 440, Baraga, MI 49908; 906-353-6651
      Twin Lakes Field Office: R 1, Box 234, Tuivola, MI 49965; 906-288-3321
   Crystal Falls Forest Area: 1420 US 2 W., Crystal Falls, MI 49920; 906-875-6622
      Wakefield Field Office: 1405 E. US 2, Wakefield, MI 49968; 906-224-2771
   Norway Forest Area: PO Box 126, US 2 W., Norway, MI 49870; 906-563-9248
      Felch Field Office: PO Box 188, Felch, MI 49831; 906-246-3245

Escanaba River State Forest (District 3):6833 Hwy 2, 41, M-35, Gladstone, MI 49837; 906-786-2351
   Escanaba Forest Area: 6833 Hwy 2, 41, M-35, Gladstone, MI 49837; 906-786-2351
      Stephenson Field Office: R 1, PO Box 31B, Stephenson, MI 49887; 906-753-6317
   Gwinn Forest Area: 410 W. M-35, Gwinn, MI 49841; 906-346-9201
   Ishpeming Forest Area: 1985 US 41 Hwy W., Ishpeming, MI 49849; 906-485-1031
      Marquette Field Office: 110 Ford Rd., Marquette, MI 49855; 906-249-1497

Lake Superior State Forest (District 4): R 1, PO Box 77, Newberry, MI 49868; 906-293-5131
   Naubinway Forest Area: PO Box 287, Hwy US 2 East, Naubinway, MI 49762; 906-477-6048
   Newberry Forest Area: Box 428, S. M-123, Newberry, MI 49868; 906-293-3293
   Sault Ste. Marie Forest Area: PO Box 798, Sault Ste. Marie, MI 49783; 906-635-5281
      Detour Field Office: PO Box 92, Detour, MI 49725; 906-297-2581
   Shingleton Forest Area: M-28, Shingleton, MI 49884; 906-452-6227
      Seney Field Office: M-28, Seney, MI 49883; 906-499-3346
      Thompson Field Office: PO Box 2555, Manistique, MI 498543; 906-341-2508

Mackinaw State Forest (District 5): PO Box 667, Gaylord, MI 49735; 517-732-3541
   Atlanta Forest Area: HCR 74, Box 30, Atlanta, MI 49709; 517-785-4251
      Alpena Field Office: 4343 M-32, Alpena, MI 49707; 517-354-2209
      Onaway Field Office: PO Box 32, M-211, R 1, Onaway, MI 49765; 517-733-8775
   Gaylord Forest Area: PO Box 667, 1732 W. M-32, Gaylord, MI 49735; 517-732-3541
      Bellaire Field Office: 701 Cayuga, Bellaire, MI 49615; 616-533-8341
   Indian River Forest Area: PO Box 10, Indian River, MI 49749; 616-238-9313
      Pellston Field Office: Box 126, Pellston, MI 49769; 616-539-8564
   Pigeon River Country Forest Area: 9966 Twin Lakes Rd., Vanderbilt, MI 49795; 517-983-4101

Pere Marquette State Forest (District 6): 8015 Mackinaw Trail, Cadillac, MI 49601; 616-775-9727
   Baldwin Forest Area: R 2, Box 2810, Baldwin, MI 49394; 616-745-4651
      Evart Field Office: 2510 US 10 E., Evart, MI 49631; 616-734-5840
   Kalkaska Forest Area: 2089 N. Birch St., Kalkaska, MI 49646; 616-258-2711
      Manton Field Office: 521 N. Michigan, Manton, MI 49663; 616-824-3591
   Traverse City Forest Area: 404 W. 14th St., Traverse City, MI 49684;616-922-5280
      Platte River Field Office: 15210 US 31, Beulah, MI 49617; 616-325-4611

AuSable State Forest (District 7): 191 S. Mt. Tom Rd., Mio, MI 48647; 517-826-3211
  Gladwin Forest Area: PO Box 337, 801 N. Silverleaf, Gladwin, MI 48624; 517-426-9205
    Harrison Field Office: 708 N. 1st St., Harrison, Mi 48625; 517-539-6411
    Standish Field Office: Box 447, 527 M-76, Standish, MI 48658; 517-846-4104
  Grayling Forest Area: 1955 N. I-75 BL, Grayling, MI 49738; 517-348-6371
    Lincoln Field Office: PO Box 122, 408 Main St., Lincoln, MI 48742;517-736-8336
    Mio Field Office: 191 S. Mt. Tom Rd., Mio, MI 48647; 517-826-3211
  Roscommon Forest Area: Box 218, Roscommon, MI 48653; 517-275-8512
    Houghton Lake Field Office: 180 S. Harrison Rd., Houghton Lake, MI 48629; 517-422-5522
    West Branch Field Office: 2389 S. M-76 West Branch, MI 48661; 517-345-0472

Cass City Forest Area: 4017 E. Caro Rd., Cass City, MI 48726; 517-872-4009
Jackson Area: 301 E. Louis Glick Hwy., Jackson, MI 49201; 517-780-7901
  Brighton Field Office: 6360 Chilson Rd., Howell, MI 48843; 313-229-5762
  Imlay City Field Office: 571 E. Borland, Imlay City, MI 48444; 313-724-4804
Grand Rapids Area: State Office Bldg., 350 Ottawa NW, Grand Rapids, MI 49503; 616-456-5071
  Muskegon Field Office: 7550 E. Messinger Rd., Twin Lakes, MI 49457; 616-788-5062
  Oceana Field Office: 1757 E. Hayes Rd., Shelby, MI 49455; 616-861-5636
  Allegan Field Office: 4590 118th Ave., Allegan, MI 49010; 616-673-5819
  Yankee Springs Field Office: 2104 Gun Lake Rd., R 3, Middleville, MI 49333; 616-795-9081

MICHIGAN BREED
AND DISCIPLINE ORGANIZATIONS

All Dressage Association of Michigan
10885 3 Mile Rd.
Plainwell, MI 49080
616-664-5077

American Driving Society
PO Box 160
Metamora, MI 48455
313-664-8666

American Saddlebred Horse
Association of Michigan
38762 Phenbrook Dr.
Farmington Hills, MI 48331
810-489-0961

Arabian Horse Association of Michigan
5201 VanOrden
Webberville, MI 48892
517-521-4242

Association of Racing Arabian Breeders
1354 N. Hillman
Stanton, MI 48888
517-831-5527

Buckskin Horse Association of Michigan
7207 W. Stoll Rd.
Lansing, MI 48906
517-626-6096

Central Michigan Cutting Horse Association
3444 Perry Rd. North
Williamston, MI 48895
313-356-3730

Great Lakes Distance Riding Association
6643 Howe Rd.
Bath, MI 48808
517-641-4622

Great Lakes Haflinger Association
1146 S. Meridian Rd.
Mason, MI 48854
517-676-5672

Great Lakes Region-US Pony Club
13550 Upton Rd.
Bath, MI 48808
517-641-6476

Great Lakes Sport Horse & Pony
3980 Morgan Rd.
Nashville, MI 49073
517-852-1584

Half-Arabian Association of Michigan
4801 Miller Rd.
Ann Arbor, MI 48103
313-994-3292

H.O.R.S.E. of Michigan, Inc.
PO Box 603
Ada, MI 49301
616-245-8517

Huron Valley Horse and Vehicle Club
313-663-2038

Lake Michigan Hunter Jumper Association
17545 Reltsema Rd.
Spring Lake, MI 49456
616-846-4772

Michigana Eventing and Dressage Assoc.
3504 W. 1650 South
Hanna, IN 46340

Michigan Appaloosa Horse Association
10899 Bunkerhill Rd.
Jackson, MI 49201
517-769-2072

Michigan Assoc. of Western Horse Club
56388 55th St.
Lawrence, MI 49064
616-674-3746

Michigan Colored Appaloosa Association
27720 72nd St.
Covert, MI 49043
616-764-8681

Michigan Combined Training Association
1766 Parnell Ave.
Ada. MI 49301
616-897-5435

Michigan Draft Horse Breeders Association
733 E. Kinter Rd.
Bronson, MI 49028
517-369-3535

Michigan Dynamometer Association
8487 Davis Highway
Lansing, MI 48917-0608
517-322-0352

Michigan Equine Practitioners Association
6607 Hart Rd.
Potterville, MI 48876
517-862-5573

Michigan Fox Trotter Association
11546 S. Nash Highway
Clarksville, MI 48815
616-693-2216

Michigan High School Rodeo Association
4717 N. Shepardsville Rd.
Elsie, MI 48831
517-862-5573

Michigan Hooved Animan Humane Society
4550 N. 38th St.
Augusta, MI 49012
616-731-5699

Michigan Horse Breeders Association
1730 N. Oxford Rd.
Oxford, MI 48371

Michigan Horse Drawn Vehicle Association
790 E. VanBuren
Alma, MI 48801
517-463-4252

Michigan Horseshoers Association
4161 E. Grand River Ave.
Bancroft, MI 48141
517-634-5679

Michigan Hunter/Jumper Association
5121 7 Mile Rd.
S. Lyon, MI 48178

Michigan Justin Morgan Horse Association
2533 Universal Dr.
Pinckney, MI 48169
313-878-6958

Michigan Mule and Jack Association
341 Fessner Rd.
Carleton, MI 48117
313-654-6822

Michigan Palomino Horse Association
010464 8th Ave. NW
Grand Rapids, MI 49504-6702

Michigan Paso Fino Club
12769 Dennison Rd.
Milan, MI 48160
313-439-8205

Michigan Quarter Horse Association
PO Box 248
Bath, MI 48808
517-641-4841

Michigan Racking Horse Show Association
8001 Merrit Rd.
Ypsilanti, MI 48197-8904

Michigan Reining Horse Association
1180 Stone Barn Rd.
Milford, MI 48380
810-887-2892

Michigan Standardbred Breeders Association
PO Box 59
Sand Creek, MI 49279
517-436-3179

Michigan State Pinto
Breeders & Owners Association
8400 E. Frances Rd.
Otisville, MI 48463
810-631-4876

Michigan State Pony of the America's Club
6955 Warner Rd.
Saline, MI 48176
313-429-9049

Michigan Trail Riders Association
1650 Ormond Rd.
White Lake, MI 48383

Michigan Welsh Pony & Cob Association
56901 11 Mile Rd.
New Hudson, MI 48165
810-437-5507

Midwest Dressage Association
16848 Towar East
Lansing, MI 48823
517-351-7304

Miss Rodeo Michigan Association
164 Zeller Dr.
Iron River, MI 49935
906-265-5610

National Barrel Horse Association
1950 64th St. SW
Byron Center, MI 49315
616-532-2150

Northern Michigan Appaloosa Regional
11295 Wolf Creek Rd.
Hubbard Lake, MI 49747

Northern Michigan Paint Horse Club
6743 Morrison Lake Rd.
Saranac, MI 48881
616-642-9753

Oakland County Sheriff Mounted Division
5783 Thomas
Oxford, MI 48371
313-628-3011

Shiawassee Trail Riders Association
33481 W. 14 Mile, Suite 100
Farmington Hills, MI 48331
810-661-5100

Southern Michigan Colored
Appaloosa Horse Club
50707 M-43
Bangor, MI 49013
616-427-7533

Southwestern Michigan Horse & Buggy Club
32018 CR 687
Bangor, MI 49013
616-427-7161

Walking Horse Association of Michigan
4516 N. Lapeer Rd.
Columbianaville, MI 48424
313-628-9288

Western Michigan Appaloosa Regional
9023 W. 74th St.
Fremont, MI 49412
616-924-3909

MICHIGAN RIDING FACILITIES
OPEN TO THE PUBLIC

Black Forest Hall, Inc.: 2787 Quick, Hoyt Rd., Harbor Springs, MI 49740; 616-526-5332; Horse college (Northwood Institute); gives English riding lessons to all ages; horses are available to ride.

Camp AuSable: Box 546, M-72 East, Grayling, MI 49738; 517-348-5491; Christian youth camp, some family weeks available; own their own horses; instruction available during summer; trail rides open to public during winter.

Chambers Riding Stable: PO Box 1326, Mackinac Island, MI 49757; 906-847-6231; general public; guide available.

Double JJ American Resort: PO Box 94, Rothbury, MI 48452; 616-894-4444; resort; trail rides for guests only; supply own horses or will board; guides available.

Double R Ranch, Inc.: 4424 Whites bridge Rd., Belding, MI 48809; 616-794-0520; resort; campground; pool; chalets; 600 acres of trails; guided; supply horses.

Douglas Meadows Ranch, Inc.: 2755 M-151, Temperance, MI 48182; 313-856-3973; open to public; supply own horses; boarding; lessons.

Five Fillies: 6660 Chilson Rd., Howell, MI 48843; 313-227-4622; open to general public; trails; summer camp; lessons; school horses.

Golden Arrow Camp: 1679 Kings Corner Rd., Mikado, MI 48745; 517-739-7800; guided western trails; will board; campground; borders the Huron National Forest.

Great Western Riding Stable North: 6394 Connell Rd., Yale, MI 48097; 810-387-3893; 313-387-2330; trail rides; basic instructions; hourly rates.

Happy Trails Stable, Inc.: 3030 12 Mile Rd., Rockford, MI 49341; 616-866-3222; summer day camp; trail riding, for hire; boarding.

Hell Creek Ranch: 10866 Cedar Lake Rd., Pinckney, MI 48169; 313-878-3632; riding stable; campground; instruction available; private instruction available; school horses; boarding.

Hunters Run: 9241 Secor Rd., Temperance, MI 48182; 313-856-2404; riding stable; board and train; lessons; summer camp; some school horses; most people bring their own.

Jack's Livery Stable: PO Box 331, Mackinac Island, MI 49757; 906-847-3391; trail rides; instruction, helmets and guides available; no boarding.

Karefree Ranch: RFD 1 Kurtz Rd., Fairview, MI 48621; 517-848-5771; riding stable; trail rides; guide; any age.

Knoblock Riding Stable: 1325 Port Austin Rd., Port Austin, MI 48467; 517-738-7228; horses for hire; guide available; no boarding.

Lakeview Stables: R 1, County Rd. 200, Roscommon, MI 48653; 517-821-6079; no instruction; guide available; 12 school horses.

Lanzor Farms: 1085 Hill Rd., White Lake, MI 48383; 810-887-1702; riding stable.

Lost Pines Stables, Inc.: 3846 W. 38 Mile Rd., Harrietta, MI 49638; 616-389-2222; school horses; guided trail rides by the hour.

Lucy's Livery: 6386 Shea Rd., Marine City, MI 48039; 810-765-9910; riding stable, trails; school horses; board, sell and lease.

Mystic Lake Camp: Box 100, 9505 Ludington Dr., Lake, MI 48632; year-round camp; school horses; instruction available; private lessons; summer camps for youth; public trail rides May-November.

Pine River Stable, Inc.: 1190 Stein Rd., St. Clair, MI 48079; 810-329-6370; trail riding.

Pineview Riding Stables: 218 Pineview, Mancelona, MI 49659; 616-585-6555; trail riding.

Pontiac Stables, Inc.: DBA Hidden Ridge Stable; 3480 Teggerdine, White Lake, MI 48386; 313-625-3410; pony and horse lessons; private and group; horseman's camp (bring your own horse); nearby campground.

Rainbow Ranch, Inc.: RFD 1, 44th Ave., New Era, MI 49446; 616-861-4445; lessons; camp; hay rides and sleigh rides; school horses.

Rolling Acres Riding Stable, Inc.: 7335 Old US 23, Fenton, MI 48430; 810-750-6455; lessons.

Silver Saddle Riding Stable, Inc.: 2991 Oakwood Rd., Ortonville, MI 48462; 810-627-2826; trail rides.

Stoney Acres Farm: 1865 M-35 Bark River, MI 49807; 906-786-3500; training; lessons; camps.

Sugar Springs Riding Stable: RFD 6, 5477 Worthington, Gladwin, MI 48624; 517-426-9958; resort; trail riding; lessons; instructor available; golf course; restaurant.

Sundown: 19950 Pratt, Armada, MI 48005; 313-784-8070; rent by the hour; school horses; instruction.

Tippicanoe Ranch: 01438 CR 687, South Haven, MI 49090; 616-637-4434; riding stable; 10 horses; guides; wooded sand dune rides.

Waterloo Riding Stable: 12891 Trist Rd., Grass Lake, MI 49240; 517-522-8920; Western lessons; hay and sleigh rides; overnight and 2-day rustic package; located in 20,000 acre park; 20 horses; 27 miles of trails; hand-led pony rides.

Wolf Lake Ranch Resort: RFD 2, Box 2514, Baldwin, MI 49304; 616-745-3890; resort; riding for guests; open on weekends 12:15-1:15 for public ride; 7-day packages; instruction available.

EQUINE HEALTH REQUIREMENTS

Inspections should be made and health certificates issued within 30 days of shipment unless otherwise specified.

STATE	SPECIAL REQUIREMENTS	HEAL CERT	NEGATIVE COGGINS TEST
AL		Yes	Yes; within 6 mos if 6 mos of age or older
AK[1]	Permit from AK 907-745-3236 AND prior approval WI 608-266-7153	Yes	Yes, within 6 mos if 5 mos or older; name of lab req'd
AZ		Yes	No, but indicate results if tested
AR	Temperature reading required.	Yes	Yes; within 6 mos if 6 mos of age or older
CA	Health cert. & $2 filing fee per animal; send fee & copy of health cert to CA State Office, 1220 "N" St., Sacramento, CA 95814 not later than date of shipment	Yes	Yes; within 6 mos; show lab and acc. number on cert; nursing foals exempt
Canada[2]	If going through Canada must also abide by Canadian requirements.	Yes	
CO	Permit req'd if EIA is pending; 303-861-1823.	Yes	Yes; within 12 mos; nursing foals under 6 mos exempt[3]
CT	Permit req'd; 203-566-4616	Yes	Yes; for auction within 60 days
DE	Temperature reading not to exceed 102°	Yes	Yes; within 12 mos; for sale of auction within 6 mos
FL	Statement req'd. "Truck to be cleaned and disinfected prior to loading	Yes	Yes; within 12 mos; name of lab req'd
GA	Temperature reading req'd not to exceed 102°	Yes	Yes; within 12 mos
HI	Call 808-941-3071; EEE and WEE vacc req'd more than 15 days prior	Yes & prior OK[4]	Yes, within 90 days; name of lab req'd; retest 45-60 days
ID		Yes	No

[1] If going through Canada, must also abide by Canadian requirements.

[2] Canada and other foreign shipments, call USDA 608-5264-5208; FTS 364-5208

[3] If accompanying dam.

[4] For prior approval, call Wisconsin Interstate (608-266-7153).

IL	Persons who consign equidae to IL race tracks and/or IL equine exhibits should contact the officials of the track or exhibit for requirements	No	No
IN	Prior approval for exhibition	Yes with 10 days	Yes; within 12 mos
IA	Name of lab req'd	Yes	Yes; within 12 months if 6 mos of age or older
KS		Yes	No
KY		Yes	Yes; within 6 mos; unweaned foals exempt for exhibition within 12 mos
LA	Name of lab and case number req'd	Yes	Yes, within 12 mos
ME	Prior approval req'd	Yes	Yes, within 6 mos
MD	Prior approval req'd	Yes	Yes; within 12 mos if 9 mos of age or older
MA		Yes	Yes; within 6 mos
MI		Yes	Yes; within 6 mos; nursing foals under 5 mos exempt
MN	Name of lab req'd	Yes	Yes; within 12 mos
MS	Copy of EIA test report with health cert	Yes	Yes; within 12 mos; copy of test report with health cert
MO	Name of lab req'd	Yes	Yes; within 12 mos; nursing foals exempt
MT	Permit req'd; 406-444-2976	Yes	No
NE	Name of lab req'd	Yes	Yes; within 12 mos; foals under 6 mos exempt
NV		Yes	No
NH		Yes	Yes; within 6 mos; nursing foals exempt
NJ	Prior approval req'd	Yes	Yes; within 30 days
NM		Yes	No
NY	Copy of EIA test report with health cert	Yes	Yes; within 12 mos if 6 mos of age or older
NC		Yes	Yes; within 6 mos

ND		Yes	No
OH	Temperature reading req'd	Yes	Yes; within 6 mos if 12 mos of age or older
OK	Name of lab desired	Yes	Yes; within 6 mos if 12 mos of age or older
OR	Permit req'd; 503-378-4710; after hours 503-873-8112	Yes	Yes; within 6 mos if 6 mos of age or older
PA	Name of lab req'd; copy of EIA test report with health cert	Yes	Yes; within 12 mos; foals under 6 mos exempt
Puerto Rico	Prior approval required; EEE and WEE vacc within 6 mos; name of lab req'd	Yes	Yes; within 6 mos
RI		Yes	No
SC		Yes	Yes; within 6 mos
SD		Yes within 10 days of shipment	Yes; within 12 mos
TN		Yes	Yes; within 12 mos if 6 mos or age or older
TX	VEE vacc req'd or permit: 512-475-6488	Yes within 10 days of shipment	Yes; within 12 mos and copy of test report with health cert or TX permit
UT	Temperature reading req'd	Yes	Yes; within 12 mos
VT	Permit req'd: 802-828-2421	Yes	Yes; within 12 mos if 6 mos of age or older
VA		Yes	Yes; within 12 mos. Sales: within 6 mos
WA		Yes	Yes; within 6 mos if 6 mos of age or older
WV	Prior approval; name of lab and temperature reading req'd	Yes	Yes; within 6 mos
WI	Name of lab req'd	Yes	Yes; within 12 mos; nursing foals exempt
WY	Name of lab req'd	Yes within 10 days of shipment	Yes; within 12 mos; nursing foals exempt